targets at which we need to shoot, because it's time for the enemy's systems to be brought down.

This book series is for every agent God has raised up to bring about the cultural transformation of nations. Charles and Liz have played a major intercessory and coaching role in my personal journey, using many of the treasures that are shared in the *Let Heaven Invade the Seven Mountains of Culture: 7M Coach Certification Guide*.

— Patrick Kuwana
Founder, Crossover Transformation Group
Johannesburg, South Africa

In this book, Dr. Robinson has pushed forward the concept of seven mountains coaching as a powerful, essential ministry. The manual is packed with practical insights, wisdom, and proven processes. Any coach considering this ministry would do well to read this book—a smaller but no less informative version of the manual.

— Dave Kahle
speaker, trainer, executive round table leader
author of *How to Sell Anything to Anyone Anytime* and other works

LET HEAVEN INVADE
The Seven Mountains of Culture

BECOME
A SEVEN MOUNTAINS
COACH

DR. CHARLES ROBINSON

↑ SPIRIT-LED
PUBLISHING

LET HEAVEN INVADE THE SEVEN MOUNTAINS OF CULTURE
BECOME A SEVEN MOUNTAINS COACH

Copyright © 2015 by WISE Ministries International
All rights reserved. No part of this publication may be reproduced, distributed, or transmitted in any form or by any means, including photocopying, recording, or other electronic or mechanical methods, without the prior written permission of the publisher, except in the case of brief quotations embodied in critical reviews and certain other noncommercial uses permitted by copyright law. For permission requests, write to the author, addressed "Attention: Permissions," at the e-mail address below:

Dr. Charles Robinson
info@coachmybusiness.com

Special discounts are available on quantity purchases by corporations, associations, and others. Orders by US trade bookstores and wholesalers—for details, contact the author at the e-mail address above.

Scripture quotations are from THE HOLY BIBLE, NEW INTERNATIONAL VERSION®, NIV® Copyright © 1973, 1978, 1984, 2011 by Biblica, Inc.® Used by permission. All rights reserved worldwide.

Editing team: Say It Well! & Inksnatcher
Cover design team: Inksnatcher & Allison Metcalfe Design
Photo of Dr. Charles Robinson: Allison Metcalfe Photography

First Edition, 2015
ISBN: 978-0-9904902-6-5
Publisher: Spirit-Led Publishing

Endorsements

Leaders need a team that can support their callings through intercession and coaching. Charles and Liz have been longtime friends and trusted intercessors for our work. I highly recommend Charles, Liz, and WISE as a valuable addition to any organization that wants to ensure that the spiritual foundation of its calling is secure.

— Os Hillman
President, Marketplace Leaders
author of *Change Agent*, "TGIF-Today God Is First," and other works

I have been researching, writing about, and leading prayer movements for twenty-five years, and I stand amazed at the ways that God has been moving leaders into exciting new areas of effective intercession and coaching for leaders. Outstanding among them are Charles and Liz Robinson, who have been breaking new ground in the area of professional spiritual services. Charles's comprehensive book will show how you, as a spiritual services provider, can benefit from this captivating and kingdom-impacting ministry. You will be glad you have this book, and you will be glad to have read it!

— C. Peter Wagner
Vice President, Global Spheres, Inc.
author of *Warfare Prayer, Acts of the Holy Spirit,* and other works

Dr. Charles and Elizabeth Robinson are ordained ministers under Christian International. They have always been passionate about their roles as ministers in the marketplace, and they have now put together a tangible series of books in order to help intercessors, coaches, and chaplains implement the powerful tools at their disposal in the seven mountains of culture. In the book *Let Heaven Invade the Seven Mountains of Culture: Become a 7M Coach,* the Robinsons have gone deep in sharing their wisdom to equip and help others minister effectively in the business world.

— Bishop Bill Hamon
Founder, Christian International Ministries Network
author of *The Eternal Church, The Day of the Saints,* and other works

I really believe in what Charles and Liz Robinson are doing, and this book describes the how-tos of a kingdom service that can really be of significant value for those arising on the mountains of society; it will help equip them for success.

— Johnny Enlow
author of *The Seven Mountain Prophecy* and other works

Dr. Charles and Liz Robinson, in *Let Heaven Invade the Seven Mountains of Culture: 7M Coach Certification Guide*, have been leaders in exposing what God is doing for his businesses at this time with his apostles, intercessors, and coaches. The link with the seven mountains, and use of an accreditation process, shows an advanced entrepreneurial flair which the body of Christ needs to embrace.

God is a businessman, and he expects us to develop the skills to bring his kingdom from heaven to earth as we pray in the Lord's Prayer. We are told many are perishing through lack of knowledge of the ways of the Father. The devil has been the one deceiving and lying to the elect wherever he can, and causing the body of Christ to be ineffective.

The roles of business apostles, professional intercessors, and coaches are still very controversial in church structures today. Accreditation and commissioning is helpful—to not only the businesses they serve, but also to being confirmed in these roles. We all can easily be discouraged before the fruit appears. We need to honor and love each other's gifting and glorify God through this.

— Dr. Stan Jeffery
Founder, Boardroom Prophets
CEO, Christ in Business Ventures, Sydney, Australia

In this end-time season, it is absolutely critical that the arrows of intercession and counsel we shoot hit the mark all the time. The prophet Jeremiah spoke these words: "Yes, prepare to attack Babylon, all you nations round about. Let your archers shoot at her. Spare no arrows, for she has sinned against the Lord" (Jer. 50:14). I personally found it amazing that the Lord released Dr. Charles Robinson to begin publish this book series in his fiftieth year, and also finalized the publishing of the first one in 2014; this further confirms the passage for me. Through this book, the Lord is giving us some very specific

I dedicate this third work to all the wonderful coaches and mentors who have been divinely equipped and empowered to speak into my life. Thank you for seeing things in me I could not see—the proof of a true coach.

I also dedicate this book to our present and future faithful and powerfully anointed seven mountains coaches—who will blanket this world's leaders with their empowering wisdom, hope, and encouragement.

Acknowledgements

Special thanks to Cathy Buettner's writing services at Say It Well! for guiding me with grace and patience on a compressed timetable. Your generosity with your Spirit-led anointing in reorganization, training, editing, and marketplace ministry transformed this work. Cathy, you are a gem!

Special gratitude to Fred and Dorinda Trick, and to all our clients and friends. Your partnerships and friendships have impacted Liz and me in ways that only God knows. This work is a testimony to the lessons learned by each of us as we have worked together.

We thank Sally Hanan of Inksnatcher, who has been a divine connection to make the final preparations on the manuscript for publishing. Your knowledge of the publishing industry and your skillsets are broad and amazing; you quickly produced excellent results. Thank you for blessing this kingdom assignment with your work.

We also thank Allison Metcalfe of Allison Metcalfe Photography and Design for how she seamlessly integrated with Inksnatcher to design and format this book's cover and interior and to insert, redo, or acquire graphics as needed to enhance the text. Her attention to detail and eye for beauty have brought these words up higher.

Table of Contents

Foreword

Preface

   1. Support & Empowerment

   2. God Needs You

   3. Coaching Defined

   4. Favor & Breakthrough

   5. Charging for Services

   6. Coaching Leaders

   7. A 7M-Enabled Coach

   8. 7M Strategies

   9. Your Choices

About the Author

More from WISE

Foreword

God is speaking to many in the church today about the role of the seven cultural mountains of influence and how strategic they are to influencing the culture for Jesus Christ. What was birthed in 1975 through Bill Bright, of Campus Crusade, and Loren Cunningham, of Youth With a Mission, is just now being realized as a core strategy to influence the culture.

We have learned that it only takes 3-5 percent of leadership operating at the top of one of these cultural spheres to actually shift the mountain—as evidenced by the gay rights movement, which has shifted the public's view of its issue by using arts & entertainment and media to reframe the public's view of it.

One of the important ingredients to this new strategy focus is the spiritual services required to prepare the soil (of leaders' hearts) for effective ministry to these seven areas. Charles Robinson, in the third volume of his new work, *Let Heaven Invade the Seven Mountains of Culture,* has given us a new resource for those called to a coaching or advisory role to leaders in the seven cultural mountains.

The Lord tells us that is it "not by might, nor by power, but by my Spirit." Prayer and godly wisdom must be at the forefront. Ezekiel 22:30 tells us that God is looking for someone to stand in the gap so that the land might not be destroyed. This book will help you understand God's strategy to affect the seven cultural mountains.

I highly recommend this resource to help you become a spiritually sound and empowering coach of leaders who affect the seven cultural mountains, so that we can restore the biblical foundations of this great nation and positively affect the nations of the world.

—Os Hillman
President, Marketplace Leaders
author of *Change Agent,* "TGIF-Today God Is First," and other works

Preface

"Those who are wise will shine like the brightness of the heavens, and those who lead many to righteousness, like the stars for ever and ever" (Daniel 12:3).

Six Assumptions I Make as I Write This for You

Assumption 1: You are a Christian and that means, for our discussion, that you have received Christ into your heart, consider yourself born again, and that you have been water baptized.

Assumption 2: You desire to serve and coach leaders in the seven mountains of culture, and you desire to equip them to fulfill their God-given calls.

Assumption 3: You are willing to extend grace and to be persistent. Please extend the grace to not let my limited vocabulary and verbiage be a blockage for you. I realize that the methods I describe in this book are unorthodox, or not what some would consider mainstream. To me, that is exactly why they work. We need new solutions to problems both old and new. I have made every attempt to make this treatise approachable and as biblically sound as possible.

Assumption 4: When I mention spiritual coaching (SC) in this book, you will think of any of the four coaching modalities. There are four paths in our 7M coaching curriculum—life coaching (foundational), spiritual coaching, executive business coaching, and executive leadership coaching. Whichever path you choose (and I recommend you explore multiple paths), know that this book will provide you with a strong foundation for your future ministry of life and spiritual coaching.

Assumption 5: You will just skip forward if the marketing language in this book turns you off. My function in WISE has been as an intercessor, salesman, marketing consultant, and the first coach to our clients (we have since added other coaches). A portion of the book markets WISE and our associated endeavors. However, I do this because it can only help you to receive a full impartation of the spirit of what we are accomplishing in the marketplace. As such, I recommend that you read everything in its entirety.

Assumption 6: You approach this topic with an open mind and a teachable spirit. You might not be charismatic in nature. but this book is still for you! We can work around our differences through grace and with a desire toward unity. Please do not let a disagreement stop you from reading this material.

Who Is This Guide For?

This guide was written to impart spiritual truth to individuals who feel called to the ministry of coaching leaders in the seven mountains. Coaches give leaders an additional spiritual advantage by empowering them for success through the coach's spiritual advice and support. We'll highlight how to identify, engage, and coach seven mountains leaders into the fullness of their corporate and familial roles, and into personal and spiritual wellness. We will also teach you how to market and teach your prospective clients the value of your coaching services and the need for the client to engage those services.

> *The WISE model utilizes the spiritual advisory team's (SAT) functions of both coach and intercessor, along with those of the corporate pastor and the chief revelatory officer (CRO).*

As a coach, you can operate as an intercessor or pastor as well, but keep in mind that each of these arenas is vastly different. For instance, all coaches need to be intercessors at times, especially when called for in a coaching session, but not all intercessors are coaches.

The Importance of Spiritual Support

You are serving Christian leaders in the seven mountains and especially in business, so you are empowering the tip of the spear. God uses you to pierce dark structures, take territory away from the ruler of the kingdom of darkness, and win that territory over to the kingdom of light. As a leader's supporter, you are surrounded by perceived and imperceived spiritual warfare. God wants to illuminate the darkness that is trying to engulf your clients and their enterprises. Scripture declares that we are not ignorant of the enemy's devices. God has given us our weapons of warfare, which are the gifts of Holy Spirit as outlined in I Corinthians 12 and 14.

You need to be supported.

While your clients are the first and best line of defense against the wiles and onslaught of the enemy, they all need help and assistance in their assignments from God. As their coach, you can minister to them one-on-one (with deliverance minsters, counselors, prophets, etc.). Your ministry times are very valuable to your clients' personal growth, emotions, and spirit. *The spiritual support team (SAT) is your client's shield of defense.*

It's also your client's offensive spiritual thrust for him, his family, his leaders, and his enterprise. His enterprise has a destiny that the SAT helps to ensure he's on track with: His enterprise needs to be where God wants it to be and do what God desires for it to do. It should impact the markets, nations, and territories God has destined it to impact.

Your Client's Enterprise

Her (or his) organization cannot be saved, but it can be sanctified—set apart for the use of the Master and the kingdom. Her enterprise can also be an impenetrable fortress of God and a force for good. Finally, her enterprise can also be a storehouse of mysteries—patents, intellectual property, and other intangible assets—and financial assets, such as lands, buildings, and other resources.

Think of your client as a modern-day Joseph

as outlined in the book of Genesis, second only to Pharaoh and over all that Egypt possessed. In the same way that Joseph directed the mass storage of grain in preparation for the seven lean years, is God calling your future clients to store up provision for his people for the coming years of lack? What part do their enterprises play in this?

Support & Empowerment

"Most intercession is in the religion mountain. How are leaders in the other six mountains to get the necessary intercession? Charles Robinson's company: WISE (Workplace Intercession, Support, Empowerment)"

— Apostle C. Peter Wagner
Vice President, Global Spheres, Inc.
author of *Warfare Prayer, Acts of the Holy Spirit* and other works

"Dr. Charles and Elizabeth Robinson have a unique perspective concerning ministry in the marketplace. Prior to their training and ordination into the ministry through Christian International, under the headship of Bishop Bill Hamon, they operated successfully in the business world and are now taking their wealth of experience to the marketplace.

As founders and originators of WISE Ministry, the Robinsons' organization provides Christian counsel and prayer covering to numerous businesses worldwide."

— Apostle Vance D. Russell,
Founder, Arise Ministries International
author of *The Kingdom* and other works

1

> *"In the last days the mountain of the Lord's temple will be established as the highest of the mountains; it will be exalted above the hills, and all nations will stream to it"* (Isaiah 2:2).

In 1975 Bill Bright, founder of Campus Crusade, and Loren Cunningham, founder of Youth With A Mission, had supper together at a conference and agreed to meet the following morning for breakfast. That night, God simultaneously gave these change agents the same dream, which they shared with each other over breakfast the following day. They saw seven mountains, which formed a larger, single mountain. God said that if they claimed the seven mountains, he would give them the large mountain, which is the kingdom of God.

The message was that if we were to impact any nation for Jesus Christ, then we would have to affect the seven spheres or mountains of society, which are the pillars of any society. These seven mountains are business, government, media, arts & entertainment, education, the family, and religion. (There are many subgroups under these main categories.) About a month later, the Lord showed Francis Schaeffer the same thing. In essence, God was telling these three change agents where the battlefield was. Here was where culture would be won or lost. Their assignment was to raise up change agents to scale the mountains and help a new generation of change agents understand the larger story.

— Os Hillman

Change Agents - What Is a Coach's Assignment?

When a coach helps business people move in line with God's heart, then the business will be more likely to succeed. Our prayer is for business owners, their families, and employees to learn to hear his heartbeat and know him in a deeper way.

On the following page there is a chart that breaks down a coach's assignment—a vital role in your client's SAT. Keep in mind that this is an abridged list. In the role of coach, you are the main point of reference with the client, while intercessors must remain anonymous. I will be discussing more of this later.

The Issachar anointing

The Issachar anointing is based on I Chron. 12:32, which states [of the numbers of the men armed for battle], "From Issachar, men who understood the times and knew what Israel should do—200 chiefs, with all their relatives under their command." In this hour, God is again raising up anointed men and women who know how to touch heaven and bring the wisdom from above down to earth on behalf of those greatly beloved by God—his coaches and intercessors in all seven mountains or spheres of society.

He is calling these anointed men and women to bring God's presence, power, and revelation to leaders outside the four walls of the church and into the marketplace. These anointed men and women, as coaches and intercessors, will lead the charge in rallying around the leaders in all seven mountains or spheres.

A Coach's Assignment
The coach will:
discover God's vision and desire for both himself and the client,
ask God for his strategy—how he wants to accomplish his vision,
report God's strategy to his overseers,
pray in agreement with the intercessor for provision and financial protection,
pray for emotional, spiritual, moral, relational, and leadership protection.
The coach:
partners with God and moves in faith to help bring God into the business,
helps the owner fulfill God's plan and vision for his or her business,
prays for the people's hearts to untie with God's heart,
partners with God and declares God's success, even when he does not see it.
The coach commits to daily:
walk in obedience to God's holy Word,
walk in purity and seek to be in unity with God and his fellow brothers and sisters in Christ,
walk in forgiveness, confession, and repentance with everyone (Ps. 51),
not allow roots of pride, bitterness, unforgiveness, or rejection to develop in his soul,
put on the whole armor of God (Eph. 6),
know his authority in Jesus's name,
proclaim God's promises in his Word for each client.

> *Their ministry will help empower, protect, and free the leaders from all kinds of bondages and hindrances, and release them into their respective destinies.*

Empowering You for Success

The sons of Issachar would go to war for the other tribes in a heartbeat. They rose early and awakened the other tribes with the sound of the shofar.[1]

> *Issachar tribe members, whose name means "wages," were the donkeys or burden bearers of their brothers.*

Issachar intercessors and coaches have ability in praying for finances and giving financial counsel. We have seen tremendous financial breakthroughs for our clients from our advice and prayers, time and time again (and even before we start praying, like the time the client's company doubled in size within twenty-four hours of signing the contract!). Can you see how your counsel can work powerfully on your client's behalf?

> "FROM ISSACHAR, MEN WHO UNDERSTOOD THE TIMES AND KNEW WHAT ISRAEL SHOULD DO—200 CHIEFS, WITH ALL THEIR RELATIVES UNDER THEIR COMMAND."
> — 1 CHRON. 12:32

Coach Within Your Mountain

The coach should be business-minded and have a background in the mountain of influence that he or she is coaching on. You are a spiritual coaching entrepreneur, a forerunner. One of the purposes of the certification course is to prepare you for dealing with finances, both in your own life and in the lives of your clients.

God is calling you, his anointed minister, to bring his presence, power, and revelation to <u>your clients</u>.

Of Issachar, their patriarch Jacob said, "Issachar is a strong donkey, crouching between the sheepfolds" (Gen. 49:14), implying the act of burden bearing again. This means that Issachar existed to help the other tribes. He was to help the sheep. Issachar, after entering into Canaan, lived in the fertile Jezreel Valley and was responsible for feeding all of the other tribes. Modern-day coaches and intercessors belong to the Issachar tribe.

As Christians, we can personally pray and apply the words from Christ's prayer, "Your kingdom come ... on earth as it is in heaven." We see an interesting corroboration of the spiritual principle in action from author John Carlson,* who relates the meanings of the names of the twelve tribes listed on the gates to New Jerusalem (in Revelation). Carlson shares that because the name Issachar can indicate intercession—seen both in the words spoken at the child's birth and the blessing Jacob gave to Issachar—intercession can allow us to enter God's kingdom and to take others in with us. The gate of intercession allows us in.

As Christ was to the multitudes, a multitude of priests will be to the world. This is a level of the unprecedented power and authority of Christ filling the earth with God's knowledge "as the waters cover the seas" (Hab. 2:14).

Jesus is, of course, the full embodiment of this priesthood.

Types of Intercessors

As the coaching part of the spiritual advisory team, it is important to recognize the various types of intercessors you may be working with on a regular basis. There are twelve types of intercessors based on the type of anointing they carry:[2]

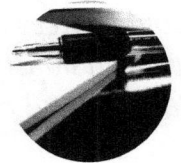

List intercessor – your personality is orderly and precise; you are faithful in completing commitments and enjoy daily covering a list in its entirety.

Personal intercessor – individuals' personal needs and one-on-one interactions motivate you.

---

* In his book, *Passion for His Presence, Entering His Gates*

Worship intercessor – you enter into the presence of God and wage warfare in the heavenlies through adoration of the Trinity.

Crisis intercessor – when you hear of accidents, tragedies, or other crises that either could happen imminently or have already transpired, something on the inside of you rises up to take action and intervene.

People group intercessor – you feel compelled to intercede for certain cultures or alienated or suppressed groups, to enter into their struggles.

Financial intercessor – you are a person motivated by the need to see God's provision in people's lives or situations; you have a proven ability to see breakthrough in your own and other people's finances.

Governmental intercessor – righteousness and justice motivate you; you are a person who honors our governmental leaders.

Mercy intercessor — you are motivated by (even unwarranted) compassion for people and their needs and failings; you weep easily over people's faults, weaknesses, and infirmities.

Issues intercessor — social causes and their injustices often anger or upset you, causing you to fervently pray.

Soul intercessor — you are outreach oriented; God uses you to bring many to him.

Warfare intercessor — conflict with the enemy excites you (this anointing is strongly related to that of a worship intercessor); you like Scriptures that talk about the vengeance of God on the head of the enemy; you find the need to walk or pace rather than sit or kneel during prayer.

Prophetic intercessor — God gives you information about other people, situations, or events; you frequently receive mental pictures about people, places, or things; what you say often comes to pass.

WISE

When God led us to form WISE™, which stands for "Workplace Intercession, Support, and Empowerment," he let us know that WISE was going to empower leaders and their employees in the marketplace by helping them fulfill their callings in their businesses and other enterprises. God gave me a corporate anointing and let me know:

> HE wanted us to take his presence and power outside the four walls of the church and into the marketplace.

> HE was going to use our business, entrepreneurial, management, and leadership skills to let heaven invade the seven mountains of culture.

God has since let us know that the "Issachar anointing" is going to be in operation in WISE, and that he is going to partner the religion mountain with all of the other mountains to:

> —fund the end-time harvest through bringing his modern-day Josephs' wisdom and discernment to multitudes, and

> —empower his people on the seven mountains for success (the inspiration for our WISE slogan: "Empowering you for success")

Our Background

At the time of this writing, we (Charles and Liz) have brought the word of the Lord to thousands of people. As experienced church and corporate pastors, intercessors, chaplains, teachers, and business owners, we and our team of intercessors, coaches, and business consultants are equipped to support and empower you and your ministry for success. In 2005 we founded a dynamic local church in Austin, Texas, where we served together as senior pastors for five years.

We are now corporate pastors to many organizations, both nationally and internationally, empowering them to impact all seven mountains of influence. We are committed to, and passionate about, training and imparting the wisdom, understanding, and experience the Lord has given us.

Our mission is to develop strong, mature ambassadors and warriors for Christ, and to bring the saving knowledge of Jesus Christ to our nation and the nations of his world.

WISE currently offers five certification courses in a series called "Let Heaven Invade the Seven Mountains of Culture."

Certification courses happen monthly. All five of the courses are available in two formats: **Group and Fast Track:** Two-and-a-half days of live on-site training; and **Independent Study:** All modules are divided over twelve weeks.

Find them here:

- markteplaceintercessors.com, marketplaceceos.com
- marketplacecoaches.com, marketplacegenerals.com
- marketplacepastors.com, corporatepastors.com

Both the group and independent study formats offered give the student impartation, wisdom, and experience from personal contact with WISE instructors.

My Prayer for You!

I pray for your seven mountains coach, Lord, that you would bless him (or her) and give him favor in the mountains and marketplaces that you have called him to. Lord, help your coach to grow his enterprise and launch out in faith into the deep.

God, I pray for a special impartation of the sevenfold Spirit of God, according to Isaiah 11:2-4: "The Spirit of the Lord will rest on him—the Spirit of wisdom and of understanding, the Spirit of counsel and of might, the Spirit of the knowledge and fear of the Lord—he will not judge by what he sees with his eyes, or decide by what he hears with his ears; but with righteousness he will judge the needy, with justice he will give decisions for the poor of the earth."

I pray that every God-given word in this book would be planted deep inside your coach and be recalled when he needs it. Lord, I pray that every ability and anointing I have would now descend upon your coach and that he would do greater works than me.

Lord, I pray for my coach's family and spouse, and for the people in his life who need protection, healing, deliverance, and who need to know someone cares and has their backs. I pray that you would open the windows of heaven right now over your coach's life and ministry, in the name of Jesus, amen!

Dr. Charles Robinson

Chapter 1: Endnotes

1. DeMain, Randy. "God is Moving Again with Holy Fire – His Manifest Presence is Coming Upon the Priesthood." www.elijahlist.com/words/display_word.html?ID=12660 (accessed June 18, 2014).

2. Femrite, Tommi, and Billie Boatwright. Intercession Workshop, Austin, TX, April, 2007. Table compiled by Cathy Buettner of Say It Well! Writing Services.

Recommended Additional Resources for Coaches

Books

> Wagner, C. Peter. *Prayer Shield: How to Intercede for Pastors, Christian Leaders and Others on the Spiritual Frontlines* Prayer Warrior Series (Book 2)
>
> Carlson, John. *Passion for His Presence, Entering His Gates*
>
> Servello, PR Mike, *God's Shield of Protection*
>
> *Intercessors - Discover Your Prayer Power* gives excellent details about each of the twelve types of anointing the Lord gives to intercessors. It lists a biblical example for each type, describing the strengths and zeals each type of anointing instills in an intercessor, and even notes pitfalls for each type and suggestions for how to avoid those pitfalls. In addition, the chapter on each intercessor type ends with a short list of five or six insightful questions, which can help intercessors discern which of the twelve types of anointing they have. *Intercessors - Discover Your Prayer Power* can be helpful to you, and is a powerful resource for those you enlist as intercessors.

Website articles

> Johnson, Nita (LaFond). "Melchizedek Priesthood." www.worldforjesus.org/articles-prophetic.php?ID=4.

DVDs/CDs

> Randy DeMain's sermons on the Sons of Issachar
> www.kingdomrevelation.org/product/sons-of-issachar

People

> Os Hillman | Marketplace Leaders
> www.marketplaceleaders.org

Elizabeth Alves, Increase International
www.increaseinternational.com About Us

Cathy Buettner, owner of Say It Well! Writing Services

Tommi Femrite, Gatekeepers International
www.gatekeepersintl.org

Billie Boatwright, Holy Ground International
www.holygroundinternational.org

Groups

Christian Business Network, Austin, TX | www.austincbn.org

International Christian Chamber of Commerce | www.iccc.net

God Needs You

"Our company has supplied equipment to contractors for more than ten years. In 2012, sales were $883,000. In 2013, sales were $1,554,000—a 76 percent increase. Why? How could we have done it again? We could not come up with anything that we or our staff had done that was responsible for more than a few percent. We had a meeting with our staff and came to the same conclusion—all of us start every day at the office by praying together. We have given the business to God, we are his shepherds, we love to give, and we partner with WISE Ministries. Charles and Liz Robinson give us ongoing personal prophecy and counseling. Their intercessory prayer team is indefatigable, and gives us written reports every two weeks on what God is saying as they pray for us. God takes good care of his own, and he gets all the glory!"

— EH, President

2

"I looked for someone among them who would build up the wall and stand before me in the gap on behalf of the land so I would not have to destroy it, but I found no one" (Ezekiel 22:30).

As a seven mountain coach, you may function in many capacities; you'll also, hopefully, be part of a spiritual advisory team that applies spiritual and strategic intelligence to the work of leaders in the seven spheres of culture. Working with an intercessor will empower every aspect of your services.

What Is Professional Level Intercession?

In this new career field called professional level intercession (named as such by apostle C. Peter Wagner), professional level intercessors (PLIs) are those trained in intercession (see volume 1). PLIs have a certain spiritual giftedness which allows them to see or hear in the Spirit, or both. They are good typists, good writers, good listeners, patient, and familiar with computer word processing software (so they can prepare intercession reports). Like coaches, these people usually have some secular skills, especially in business or via involvement in the seven mountains, such as video editing, teaching, business accounting, producing—any skillset or experienced background that would give them special insight or authority to pray. A pastor who wants to increase church income could minister to local businesses and other

enterprises by offering the services of PLIs and coaches. PLIs can be on the church staff list in the same way that retired ministers or part-time counselors are. You get it, you name it. The PLI or 7MCPC designation should be up there with CPC, CPA, DM, MBA, etc. The training and experience is no less rigorous, and the spiritual warfare can get very interesting as well!

You, and other spiritual team members, will interface with your clients and (potentially) with their other leaders and family members. The SAT will create a spiritual climate in which the client and his organization can have maximum protection from the enemy. You'll help your client learn how to receive his assignment(s) from the Lord and communicate his message clearly to his target market. He will work with the direction the Lord gives him and his spiritual team, and follow it for his enterprise and personal daily life.

Helping leaders hear the voice of God better[1]

WISE does not come in and tell a client how he should run his enterprise or manage his employees. However, after trust is built, the consulting arm of what we do can get involved with personnel issues and strategic directional issues. WISE exists to help clients better discern and know the voice of God for themselves. WISE becomes a sounding board for them to confirm that they really do hear the voice of the Lord—the voice of God sounds like their thoughts, but there is a subtle spark of divine inspiration that WISE has which can help them learn to discern and detect. We have found that our leaders greatly increase in this ability to hear the voice of God, since that is one of our main giftings.

"My sheep listen to my voice; I know them, and they follow me" (John 10:27).

It's a privilege for all of God's people to hear his voice, but we all can hear more clearly as we exercise this gift. The job of WISE intercessors (and more for coaches) is to be our clients' cheerleaders. We are there to encourage leaders to pursue the Lord's voice and to help build their faith. God wants to build a platform for our SATs to minister to clients and their leaders, both in person *and* from behind the scenes.

Why Pray?

Prayer is the single most powerful force for change in the universe. E.M. Bounds, a noted prayer warrior, said,[2]

"Prayer is the greatest of all forces, because it honors God and brings Him into active aid."

He also stated,

"Everything depends on prayer, and yet we neglect it not only to our own spiritual hurt but also to the delay and injury of our Lord's cause upon earth. The forces of good and evil are contending for the world. Had there been persistent, universal, and continuous prayer by God's people, long ago this the earth would have been possessed for Christ."

God allows us to partner with him in prayer to change situations. Someone may ask, "God is sovereign, so why do I need to pray?" The answer is that God, in his sovereignty, restricts himself to the limits of our partnership with him in prayer. God directs us, but we respond in prayers that bring heaven to earth. The will of God expressed through us, and the words spoken, bring to earth not only the will of God, but also *the manifestation of what we are praying about*—for us *and* you. How does intercession differ from prayer?

The differences between prayer and intercession

When you combine focused and targeted intercession (a higher form of prayer) for enterprises in all seven mountains of society, you can change any aspects or elements of society for good at their cores.

> **Prayer** is the act of obedience in bringing feelings and desires—words from our hearts—to life.
>
> **Intercession** denotes the carrying of a burden that is from God's heart.

We can pray about anything in our hearts, but to intercede means that we choose to stand in the gap for someone or something (e.g., a cause).

In intercession, we choose to become identified with that cause or individual. The intercessor carries a burden of the Lord which oftentimes is not released from him until that which he has been given to speak, and in some cases suffer, has been accomplished."*†

---

* Intercessors can obviously be both men and women.
† The table on page 17 gives even more characteristics of the differences in prayer and intercession.

Our own Holy Spirit intercedes for us in sounds that cannot be uttered: "In the same way, the Spirit helps us in our weakness. We do not know what we ought to pray for, but the Spirit himself intercedes for us through wordless groans" (Rom. 8:26). Jesus, himself, never ceases to make intercession for us at the right hand of the Father, as Scripture states in Romans 8:34: "Who then is the one who condemns? No one. Christ Jesus who died—more than that, who was raised to life—is at the right hand of God and is also interceding for us."

Opposition to the WISE model

Our company history illustrates that professional level intercession works, and this is why we heavily recommend that a leader not only receive coaching from WISE, but that he also receive professional intercessory services. Think about our track record. How could WISE be in business since 2005 in this challenging economy (and our services are not cheap) if this service did not work? Not only have we been able to remain in business, this ministry has been our main source of full-time employment since 2005. When talking with Lance Wallnau, Lance stated that "many have tried this field and have not been successful in it, but you have; congratulations!" Our success is due to our model and calling.

Many years ago, I received a prophecy that stated, "You have a message that is going to go far and wide in the earth." I believe that this book, and the others in this series, is the vehicle to get that message to the world.

The Lord often encourages us by having our clients acknowledge the powerful effects of our prayers. In one case, the intercession was so much a part of the increase that the leaders of the company got together and tried to reason how this increase had actually happened. The only deduction they could make was that it was because of the prayer! Yay God! (I must be careful to not take credit where credit is really due to the Lord; he is the one responsible, while the intercessors were his vessels.)

Review: sons of Issachar anointing

The sons of Issachar were people of action—*servants* to their brothers in the other tribes, and were not looking for their own gain.

> **THEY** have spiritual intelligence and are faithful, obedient servants whom God is raising up, and whom God can trust.

Prayer	Professional Level Intercession
I will pray for you if I remember.	I will intercede for you at regular intervals.
I maybe only know a general need.	I will intercede for you according to knowledge of your life, family, and business(es).
I am a generalist.	I am a specialist.
I do not follow up with you.	I follow up and ask for status updates regularly.
I do not show you that I prayed.	I produce a report for you on what I prayed.
I speak to God; I do not ask him for specifics about you or your situation.	I ask God what he has to say about the situation, then listen and record specifics he gives me about you and your situation.
I may not pray for you for several weeks.	I pray for you 2-3 times per week.
I may be praying for old, answered requests. I do not follow up with you to see if the prayers were answered.	I pray for only current, valid needs. I will follow up and will stop praying/pray for other issues when I am notified that the prayers were answered.
You do not know what I am praying.	You know exactly what I am praying since I write down my prayers for you.
I cannot hear God speak clearly to me about you.	I hear God speak to me every day about you and others, as I am gifted in this area.
I pray in my spare time.	I intercede in my dedicated time.
I do not get paid for this.	I get paid well and look forward to my time on your behalf.
I pray for maybe 1-3 minutes for each need.	I intercede for 30-60 minutes at a time.
My prayers are limited to the one or two topics that you mentioned.	My intercession is comprehensive; we put eight powerful prayer shields around you and your loved ones. We pray for important meetings, travel, spouse, children, other leaders, and your important business clients.

This table lists characteristics of the current mindset about prayer compared to the characteristics of professional level intercession. The table illustrates how professional level intercession is at an entirely higher level than regular prayer, and carries with it the expectation of results.

THEY build others up rather than try to build up their own ministries.

THEY have the heartbeat of God and the frequency of heaven.

THEY love God; through obedience they are willing to fight to the death for the people to whom they are assigned.

Clients - this is your job

It is to find these anointed sons of Issachar and engage them, inform them, release them, and bless them; then watch the favor and breakthrough that happens in lives, families, and in all endeavors!

Jesus said "A servant is not greater than his master" (John 15:20). The job of your spiritual coaches and intercessors is not to tell you, the leaders in your enterprises, what to do. You are to partner with those who are in the Issachar tribe, who will act as a sounding board and help fine-tune your spiritual ears to hear God's voice.

Many are shifting gears in this season; are you shifting up or down? (If shifting down, remember the slingshot principles. The more you pull back, the farther you'll go, i.e., the more you rest and recharge, the further you'll go.) What is your organization's pace for this year?

God Needs Coaches and Intercessors!

Ezekiel 22:30 says "I looked for someone among them who would build up the wall and stand before me in the gap on behalf of the land so I would not have to destroy it, but I found no one." This is an unfortunate and sad situation. God looked for someone to stand in for the *land* that he would not have to destroy it. He could find no one.

Godly leaders from all walks of life are exposed; the enemy has broken through the wall/hedge or, even worse, there was never any wall and God's people are being plundered by the enemy. People are going to hell, profits are being squandered, companies are going out of business, marriages are breaking, and children are being taken captive at the enemy's will, all because there is *no hedge*. There are *no intercessors and few kingdom coaches!*

We aim to change that. We and our faithful team members have dedicated our lives—since 2005—to protect, empower, and advise these precious ones so that the work of the enemy in their lives would cease, and that these leaders would fulfill their divine callings from God and reach a level of actualization and fulfillment they never would have known without the coaching, mentoring, and intercession WISE's team provided.‡

As your intercessors pray and intercede for your clients, they become the first line of defense for him, his business, and his family.

These are lifelong relationships God has sovereignly initiated. We, they, and God take what we do very seriously. God told me to make my leaders bulletproof, which is exactly what we do through Holy Spirit. Leaders are taken through our novel coaching and mentoring program of inner healing and discipleship (in the seven mountains). Their businesses are empowered to be as important to God as the local churches in their regions. Their enterprises become *outposts* for the kingdom of God in those territories, with angels of war assigned to them. Their land becomes the *habitation* of angels, and their enterprises become *tools in the hand* of God for their regions, as well

---

‡ Access the DVD "Intercession 2.0, Going from Intercession to Intervention." In it I relate God's plans to principles from the science of physics. See a store link on page 112.

as for the people of their regions. Salvations occur when people walk into their businesses; people are knocked down by the power of God while walking into their establishments. Negotiations become much easier because of the presence of Holy Spirit. Favor falls and business expands effortlessly. I remember we had one company double in size within twenty-four hours upon signing the contract, and we had not even started praying! The blessing occurred because they had become *apostolically and prophetically aligned* with us. In many of our companies, we experience more of the power of God than we do in our churches. I am not putting down the church. Jesus loves his bride, but the warfare in the marketplace is greater than the warfare in the church, so we need more of God's power there.

Back to the passage: there is no one to stand in the gap, to make a hedge or wall—a first line of defense against the *wiles,* attacks, and deception of the devil. Eph. 6:11 tells us to take on the full armor of God to resist the devil's plans. Leaders of all types need to be taught *how* to stand (the purpose of our God's Generals Certification Course).

As you coach, listen to, understand, and spend time with your clients, you become the first line of defense for them, their businesses, and their families. The enemy is going to have to go through *you* and the agape love you have for your clients to get to them. That is why you must be strong in the Lord, know him, and be experienced in spiritual warfare. There is no room for novices here. With your WISE team, you have the experience and the knowledge to provide everything your client needs to succeed, which has been proven in all seven mountains.§

Remember, if it is only you coaching and there are no intercessors (an option for a financially challenged client), then you will be doing

---

§ Perhaps you want to learn more about our intercession training. WISE offers certification training on that topic (volume 1 in this series), whereby you can earn the designation CPI (Certified Professional Intercessor).

some praying, especially in the coaching session—usually at the beginning and at the end of each session. You decide what to propose in the initial consult based upon the client's answers to the survey questions.

You may also operate in the capacity of corporate pastor, although having another individual perform this function is preferable. The corporate pastor function (another name for a chaplain, but the CP may have additional responsibilities) is to minister to the needs of the employees.

Doors Unlocked for YOU

The relationship between king and prophet, if you will, can produce the things the Lord has promised you, and you can see those great and mighty prophetic words fulfilled through the relationships that are established between you and the rest of your client's spiritual advisory team. In many cases, these are lifelong journeys that you will travel on together. If you can *see* it, you can *have* it. This career and this training is the manifestation or the *key* to what God has been promising you all these years, and the precious fruit of these God-ordained relationships will last forever!¶

Convergence

When all the life lessons, tests, wisdom gained, and cumulative experiences come together to empower you for the main assignment of your life, you reach convergence. You will enter convergence, and with your spiritual advisory team, you will empower your clients to be in convergence as well."

> Do you know that only 20 percent of leaders in the body of Christ ever enter into convergence in the work that God has called them to do? Being in convergence is the secret to getting to the top of anything."
> — Dr. Lance Wallnau, *The Seven Mountain Strategy*

¶ See the text "What Is a Destiny Link?" a term coined by Sandie Freed, for more discussion on the relationship aspect of this ministry.

Chapter 2: Endnotes
1. WISE Ministries. "Services." www.coachmybusiness.com/services-main.php
2. Bounds, E.M. *Classic Collection on Prayer*. Sydney: ReadHowYouWant, 2011.
3. WISE Ministries. "Intercession for Christian Leaders." www.coachmybusiness.com/Intercession_for_Christian_Leaders_2.pdf (accessed June 4, 2014).

Recommended Additional Resources for Coaches
Books

> Hillman, Os. *The 9 To 5 Window: How Faith Can Transform the Workplace*
>
> Hamon, Bill. *Prophetic Scriptures Yet to Be Fulfilled: During the 3rd and Final Reformation*
>
> Wagner, C. Peter. *Prayer Shield: How to Intercede for Pastors, Christian Leaders and Others on the Spiritual Frontlines* Prayer Warrior Series (Book 2)
>
> Alves, Beth, Tommi Femrite, and Karen Kaufmann. *Intercessors - Discover Your Prayer Power*
>
> Freed, Sandie. *Destiny Thieves: Defeat Seducing Spirits and Achieve Your Purpose in God*

Website articles

> Wallnau, Lance."How to Crack the Code that Unlocks You." www.lancelearning.biz/crack-the-code.

DVDs/CDs

> Randy DeMain's sermons on the Sons of Issachar www.kingdomrevelation.org
>
> Lance Wallnau, "Take All 7" 4 DVD series, www.lancelearning.com
>
> Os Hillman, Lance Wallnau, and others "7 Mountain Strategies: Keys for Cultural Influence" Audio CD Series, www.7culturalmountains.org

People
> Lance Wallnau | www.lancewallnau.com
> Sandie Freed | www.sandiefreed.com

COACHING DEFINED

"Charles, you gave me a word that a credit was coming to me from a lawyer. Out of the blue, a lawyer contacted me two weeks later with a surprise credit that was due to my wife from over two years ago. It was enough to cover our rent that was due in days. Praise God."

— SHC, Calgary, AB

"I could have saved myself a lot of misery over the years by watching out for those who had my back. I more than ever realize the importance of certain intercessors in certain places. I understand that having the wrong people praying for you can hinder the things God wants to do in your life. Many of these things I learned the hard way, so take Charles's information to heart and save yourself a lot of distress, financial losses, as well as setbacks that could probably have been avoided by properly surrounding yourself with a strong hedge of defenses."

— Bill Smith
CEO, Now Enterprises, Inc.

3

"I have told you these things, so that in me you may have peace. In this world you will have trouble. But take heart! I have overcome the world"(John 16:33).

"The prayer of a righteous person is powerful and effective" (James 5:16b).

Coaching Vs. Intervention

As a coach in the seven mountains, you want your clients' spiritual destinies to be clear to both them and the world. Is the destiny of your clients' enterprises being interfered with, distorted, or cancelled out; or is it getting through with clarity and consistency and being reinforced?

Prayer is *not* enough; your clients *also* need intervention—yours and God's. The answers and direction they need are already inside them, and it's up to you to draw it out. They also need your advice, counsel, and wisdom—people to come alongside them and share from their experience. By listening well and not interrupting when they are talking—half of what you do—you help and encourage your clients to make courageous choices, the choices that Jesus would have them make.

The enemy will try to confuse or distort your client's message, possibly through miscommunication, or by combining some of the world's philosophies with your client's personal misperceptions, leading him to market a mixed message about his product or service.

You and the PLI can help run interference on the enemy's interference, thus neutralizing his effect on your client and his enterprise.

Often, the spiritual intelligence we need requires that we go from plain intercession (reactive) to intervention by running interference (proactive). We do it in the same way that football offensive fullbacks and tight ends run ahead of a halfback as he carries the ball and block prospective tacklers out of the way. It could also be compared to the way your defensive players run interference for your teammates if one of them takes possession of the ball when your team is on defense. Interference can also mean the act of illegally hindering an opponent from catching a forward pass or a kick.

You are going ahead of your clients in the Spirit and blocking the enemy so they can move forward. *When you run interference, you stop being passive and become active* in clearing the airwaves. PLIs and coaches run interference on the enemy. Say this out loud:

"I run interference on the enemy."

Your clients have a message to receive from God. Their potential business clients have a message to receive from them. It's simple: clear up the communication channels to enhance their messages!

Interference also pertains to linguistics. If there is a lot of babbling in your clients' industries, how can you help them stand apart? The enemy may be trying to confuse or distort their messages. Are their messages getting out or is there overlap and miscommunication?

We can break up all interference in the heavenly realm, which will then see its parallel in the earthly realm.

> *Your enterprise is a tool of heaven to bring transformation to your region and sphere of influence, and it is specifically that destiny that Satan will try to block.*

All who are working for the advancement of God's kingdom come into spiritual opposition from God's enemy—the devil and his minions. The enemy would like distort the truth and cause your clients and their SAT teams to have difficulty receiving the clear messages of God for their assignments.

Three steps for a coach to bring clarity to his client's message

Your client can have a full release of her divine purpose if she has a clear channel of communication to God. It allows the clear message of her products or services to convey her enterprise's spiritual destiny to her intended audience (there is no weakening, distortion, or cancellation—think of a bad radio signal). Her SAT team can use a three-pronged strategy to approach this.

1. Use offline intercession and decrees (intervention) to "clear the airwaves" over her enterprise.
2. Go from a passive role in the quantum realm to an active role (interference).
3. Use coaching to develop your client's personal spirit and habits to be more in tune with God through the Word, inner healing of emotional issues and self-defeating behavior, and the infilling of the Spirit of God.

Helping your client hear and communicate the truth of her enterprise's spiritual destiny is an important part of the professional seven mountains coaching she receives.

Knowing who you are in Christ—knowing your identity—unlocks your destiny.

What Is Life Coaching?

Life coaching is all about helping people get from where they are in their lives to where they want to be. If we are all honest with ouselves, we know we could do with improving an area or two of our lives. We *know* what to do to become more successful, but we don't do what we know. Life coaches help bridge the gap between where you are and where you want to be.

It is a life coach's job to help people get what they want in life by breaking down the barriers that they impose on themselves. WISE combines traditional coaching with counseling to produce a hybrid model that has proven very effective. Christian life coaches serve their clients through the love of Jesus Christ in a faith-based, biblical approach.

The Role of a WISE-Certified 7M Spiritual, Life, or Executive Coach

Rather than actually *telling* someone the answers, a WISE 7MCPC is the catalyst for helping a client find the answers himself. By asking challenging and thought-provoking questions, a coach can unlock a client's potential.

Coaching is forward looking and focused on the actions a client is willing to take to get what he wants out of life.

Sometimes your mentee can't see the forest through the trees. He is so wrapped up in everyday life that it just passes him by! Coaching enables him to take a step back and actually examine his life and *all* of its components (not forgetting the spiritual components). This leads to greater self-awareness, focus, and accountability.

Spiritual and life coaching - what is it?

All spiritual and life coaching methods are not created equal! There are at least three broad approaches to coaching based upon one's worldview. The first is a purely secular approach that attempts to unlock the person's human potential. Techniques used may be such methods as neurolinguistic programming (NLP), etc. The second takes a non-Christian spiritual approach to "enlightenment," and may be combined with the first. It harnesses components of the New Age movement, such as the divine nature being present within the person who has not acknowledged Christ. The third is a Christian approach, which utilizes the God-given gifts within the person and acknowledges the need of Holy Spirit in achieving greater results.

All spiritual/life coaching is *not* the same; it can incorporate elements of humanistic and New Age teaching. Unlike the New Age movement, the guided visualization and meditation techniques we use are only guided by God's Spirit to show us things of him. [Your imagination is your connection to heaven or hell, light or darkness, depending on how it is used and what it is connected with.] We believe that the human spirit can only achieve enlightenment and actualization through a Romans 12:2 transformation of the mind after a true born-again experience.

This coaching is combined with the knowledge of God's perfect will for your client. We tap into her gifts, which will propel her into accomplishing her destiny. This is called being in the flow—that feeling of being 100 percent alive and operating on "all cylinders," if you will.

How does coaching work?

Spiritual, life, and executive coaching can be done in person, on the telephone, or using e-mail (although phone coaching is impersonal and not recommended). Group coaching can be done in person (WISE Masterminds and Round Tables), over the phone (tele-class), or online.

During each coaching session, you and your client will discuss and explore his journey. You'll include his goals, wins, challenges, frustrations, and opportunities, as well as develop fieldwork for the coming week.

Fieldwork isn't like the homework you were assigned in school—it consists of action steps to move your client closer to the realization of his goals and dreams. He brings the agenda and you bring the coaching skills to create a partnership that moves him forward, all in the framework of 7M marketplace ministry.

No matter which of the four types of coaching you offer, you are referred to as your client's SC. You and your client schedule coaching sessions that are usually biweekly and last from a half hour to an hour. Endeavor for sixty minutes, as this is a standard duration for counseling and other professional sessions. Go for no more than seventy-five minutes.

Some clients may prefer a weekly meeting in order to grow faster and build a strong coach-client relationship with you. Sessions may be focused on one specific goal or challenge, or on a much broader set of personal or professional issues. Their lives can be powerfully changed through your Christian life coaching gift.

Spiritual Coaching

Spiritual coaching focuses on your client's inner life and time spent with God, along with certain books of the Bible that highlight wisdom and self-discipline. Spiritual coaching also helps activate your client by identifying his unique makeup of personality, gifts, anointings, and dreams, and then emphasizing their use in everyday life.*

---

* An activation is the calling forth of a spiritual gift or talent that is latent. Activations realize and release what is being called forth.

Clients will discover their ministry, the major gifts of Holy Spirit they operate in, the five-fold ministry gift(s) they have a natural bent for, and how it all relates to marketplace ministry in all seven mountains of culture. Profile assessments are used throughout the process, such as the DISC and the spiritual gifts inventories. Not only can an individual go through this process, but also the leaders and employees in the organization. It will better help them appreciate each other's gifts and talents and foster closer teamwork.

A faith-based life coach is

- a personal life trainer to enable clients to achieve their goals,
- a champion and cheerleader during a turnaround and transition,
- a trainer in communication and life skills,
- a sounding board when making important choices,
- a motivator when strong actions are called for,
- unconditional support when clients take a hit,
- a mentor in personal self-development,
- a co-designer when creating an extraordinary project,
- a beacon and friend during stormy times,
- a wake-up call if clients don't hear their own,
- a partner in helping clients have all of what matters most to them.

Life coaching *is the foundation of what we do as coaches, and deals with the basic issues of life—relationships, goals, personal issues, hang-ups, etc.*

Spiritual coaching *deals with your inner life and relates to your walk with the triune God. In this discipline, we help you to better hear the voice of God, to relate more deeply to the godhead, etc.*

Executive-Level and Executive Leadership Coaching

Executive-level coaching is further subdivided into executive business and executive leadership coaching. In this discipline we deal with helpful tools for the leader's life such as time management, leadership development (both for the executive and for his or her team), communication styles and methods, 360 evaluations, etc.

Executive coaching is becoming more of an integral necessity for executives in leadership roles.

Coaching often relieves the loneliness at the top, which CEOs and their counterparts experience when dealing with the complex issues resulting from their decisions and actions. Egos, ethics, and perceptions that ultimately influence the stakeholders of a company require the introspection executive coaching can bring.

Executive coaches can address needs in leadership development, speech delivery, business etiquette, people skills, management, and even appearance. It may be necessary to have coaches who specialize in these different elements.

Why senior executives hire certified coaches as consultants

To observe their performance and give feedback. Impartial feedback is less threatening from a consultant coach.

The time and attention of the coach is devoted solely to maximizing the leader's time, balancing work life, and creating new and improved behaviors and habits, thus benefiting most aspects of his enterprise.

Coaches have an appropriate business background, are experienced in coaching skills, and are able to administer appropriate assessment tools.

Coach certification guarantees a specific level of competence. (This is the purpose of our 7MCPC certification.)

Group Coaching/Mastermind/Round Tables

Group coaching cannot start until you have, say, six to twelve people. It is usually for a defined time, such as six or twelve months. Everyone knows when the sessions start and end. Can they be done over the Internet or live? I much prefer live.

In a mastermind group there is usually a focus, such as building your business or start-up.

Round tables can be for established organizations. Leaders meet usually once a month for four to eight hours.[†]

Training vs. coaching

Coaching skills are also used to train; however, it is important to know when to train and when to coach. The following table compares/contrasts the two, relative to your client's desired outcomes.

The WISE master offerings list has all of the services and trainings that WISE offers—coaching, intercession, inner healing, and counseling—as well as our spiritual gifts intensive trainings. We will cover all these in our certification course.

Training	Coaching
Imparts skills	Applies skills
Helps break old habits	Helps build new habits
Encourages new behaviors	Creates new behaviors
Narrows employee's range of freedoms	Widens range of freedoms
Requires supervision	Decreases supervision
Builds knowledge	Builds people
Learning focused	You determine the focus
Structured, gives resources	Accesses and activates your resources
Teaches about vision	Brings forth your vision
Focuses on your development	Encourages your development

[†] See WISE Round Tables, Truth @Work, Convene, Pinnacle forum, etc.

WISE coaches

WISE coaches are coaches first and counselors second. I have coined the term "coachelor" for this. Traditional coaching models do not tie coaching in with counseling—they just try to get to the end result or goal, but we at WISE know that there are spiritual roots to many issues in life, so we do both. [If you are a licensed counselor, however, you know that you will need to establish strict boundaries between your coaching and counseling practices.]

Many Christians are prone to live and experience their Christian walk through head knowledge. We help people relate to the Lord and to each other at the heart level. What are your client's relational skills? How can you help her improve them?

The word coach has its origins in transportation—a conveyance to take you from where you are to where you want to go. That's exactly what we can do together. Einstein famously defined insanity as doing the same thing over and over again yet expecting a different result each time. If people are stuck, sliding backwards, or moving forward just too frustratingly slowly, it may be time for them to find a coach to mentor, challenge, and help launch them to the next level.

Go get 'em, tiger!

Chapter 3: Endnotes

Recommended Additional Resources for Coaches

Books

> Hillman, Os. *The 9 to 5 Window: How Faith Can Transform the Workplace*
>
> Hamon, Bill. *The Day of the Saints: Equipping Believers for Their Revolutionary Role in Ministry*

Website Articles

> Washington Post. "The Average Work Week is Now 47 Hours." www.washingtonpost.com/blogs/on-leadership/wp/2014/09/02/the-average-work-week-is-now-47-hours/

People

> Tony Stolzfus, Leadership Metaformation | www.meta-formation.com

Groups

> Christian Business Network, Austin, TX | www.cbnaustin.org

FAVOR & BREAKTHROUGH

"As the founder and CEO of a company that reaches directly into all seven mountains of culture, including nearly half of all Fortune 100 corporations, our partnership with WISE Ministries has been invaluable. We would not be as effective, nor have the influence that we do, without its support and friendship."

— Randy S., Washington State

"Charles and Liz Robinson of WISE have the knowledge, the heart, and the experience to provide intercessors for business. Because of our excellent experiences as their clients, I hope the Robinsons continue to disciple many more intercessors. We know firsthand how gifted the Robinsons are, since, from 2005, we have both watched them shepherd their employees, and benefited from their guidance for us as we steered our business through many adventures.

Simply said, Charles and Liz Robinson were given to us by God, who knew that we needed the friendship, mentoring, and spiritual authority they possess to move forward in his purposes—not only in our business life but also in our personal walks with him. They are the real deal, and operate in the true anointing of Father because of the level of intimacy they each keep with him. They are our friends, comrades-in-arms in spiritual warfare, and our spiritual mentors all in one!"

— Reverend Dorinda Trick
counselor

4

"And see if I will not throw open the floodgates of heaven and pour out so much blessing that there will not be room enough to store it" (Malachi 3:10).

The Joseph Experience

God is raising up many leaders in the field of marketplace ministry through "Joseph" experiences. Os Hillman has written much about this phenomenon, in which the Lord takes a Christian in the seven mountains through a difficult time of testing. Christian leaders may lose most or all material possessions and/or relationships in the process of refining their total dependence on God. In the process, the "Joseph" Christians may also go through several tests to see if their character is mature enough for the leadership positions the Lord is preparing them to have in the coming moves of God in the seven mountains.

Why is the marketplace such a critical area for ministry? Rich Marshall, author of *God@Work* and *God@Work2*,[1] feels the Scripture has been fulfilled in the Bible verse Luke 10:2: "The harvest is plentiful, but the workers are few. Ask the Lord of the harvest, therefore, to send out workers into his harvest field." Rich relates how, in the United States as well as other countries, more workers are not Christian than are Christian. However, Christians from many different denominations (the workers) are spread throughout the workforce among the unbelievers (the harvest fields). Those workers have learned how to work together in their jobs; getting them to work together for kingdom purposes is just the next step we need to accomplish for the sake of what God has planned for the seven mountains.

Cities of Gold

While going through a SOZO inner healing session,* Holy Spirit told me that he wanted to take me to meet someone. He led me to a sea of hot coals. I could see Jesus in the distance. Jesus said I was to walk across the hot coals and to take my shoes off before walking. I said "I cannot, Lord, it will burn me!" Jesus assured me that I could do it. I took my shoes off and walked across.

Next, I came upon a river of fire. Jesus was very close now, but there was no way I could go through that river; Jesus knew this was too much for me, so he stood up on his throne and reached out. (His arms became extremely long; he lifted me up over the river of fire and plopped me right on his lap!) Jesus then showed me a dark city. He threw a handful of gold and the city lit up with an amazing show of light, color, and splendor. Then he repeated the same action over another city, then another. He spoke to me and said, "Charles, I have called you as a Joseph to the sheep nations and cities." The vision ceased.

I had to go through the river of fire to reach that point. "They strengthened the disciples in these cities and encouraged the disciples to remain faithful. Paul and Barnabas told them, 'We must suffer a lot to enter the kingdom of God'" (Acts 14:22 GWT).

The visions all unite to explain Josephs together forming a patchwork

Several months after the cities of gold experience, I was sitting in my office when I "saw" myself at an ironing board. I was ironing a nondescript fragment of cloth that was incomplete by itself; it had a definite color (green) and a definite texture. It was thick, appearing to be made of a heavenly substance I could not identify. It was almost as if the piece of cloth were my own life and I was processing it … ironing out the wrinkles. I was feeling alone, feeling I was not making much of an impact. The vision expanded: I saw many other Josephs ironing out the fabric of their lives, ironing out the wrinkles in circumstances and relationships, seemingly feeling alone and in obscurity. Next, I saw a most amazing mantle, a garment. Each piece of fabric was now sewn into each of the other pieces. Even though there were numerous colors and countless types of fabrics and textures, each piece fit together into the garment perfectly. These

---

* SOZO is the Greek word translated "saved, healed, delivered." Sozo ministry is a unique inner healing and deliverance ministry aimed at getting to the root of things hindering your personal connection with the Father, Son, and Holy Spirit.

individual pieces were not symmetrical, but all shapes and sizes, yet when they were fitted together, not one piece overlapped the boundaries of another and there was not one gap in the garment. It was splendid! There was no lack; everything had been provided for by God and his Josephs—solutions, inventions, creativity, provision, protection—and the mantle covered it all! I discovered that this, the fabric of our lives, was Joseph's coat of many colors which will be worn by all of the Josephs, universally, in this final hour. I subsequently did some research on Joseph's coat and learned that one reference[4] said it was a patchwork quilt.

This became the theme of our Tipping Point Unconference in 2013—the coat and a new anointing for that patchwork quilt. The patchwork quilt is what God is birthing through us—his Josephs and the intercessors and coaches who support the Josephs. (Note that the intercessors and coaches who support the Josephs shall themselves also become Josephs.) The patchwork quilt provides all that is needed.

There is a new wisdom and a new anointing for the times in which we live. Daniel 12:3 states that in the latter days "those who are wise will shine like the brightness of the heavens."

You are called to shine in this new career field.

Many will come to the Lord's light. This wisdom is called the Daniel or Joseph anointing. God's righteousness, character, and integrity will shine through us in the midst of a very great darkness (see Is. 61), and we will reflect his glory as the moon reflects the light of the sun at night. In the way that Joseph had the answers when Pharaoh asked him for the interpretation of his dream,[†] we will have the answers and interpretations when the questions are asked. The problems which will face us are of an order of magnitude greater than any problems that have faced us previously.

---

† Of the seven fat cows and the seven skinny cows that ate the fat cows (see Gen. 37-50)

Spiritual Gates

We will open spiritual gates, because we will also have the *solutions*—heavenly, great, and ingenious ones, the number of which will have greater impact than those which came before. Angels reserved from the foundation of the world will be released. We will operate as a modern-day Jacob's ladder which stretches to heaven—one upon which the angels ascend and descend. Most importantly, the Lord is at the top of the ladder directing the angelic activity (even over your life).

> Jacob ... had a dream in which he saw a stairway resting on the earth, with its top reaching to heaven, and the angels of God were ascending and descending on it. There above it stood the Lord ... When Jacob awoke from his sleep, he thought, "Surely the Lord is in this place, and I was not aware of it." He was afraid and said, "How awesome is this place! This is none other than the house of God; this is the gate of heaven" (Gen. 28:10-17).

Jacob named that place Bethel, which means "house of God." He redefined the purpose of that place.

Warfare to open and close gates

God uses WISE Ministries to open portals (or gates/windows/doors) and to displace forces of darkness over enterprises, cities, regions, and territories.

Gates are very strategic.

The enemy understands this as well. Warfare is ongoing in the seven mountains, more heavily in some mountains than in others. Ruling spirits fight to open and close gates of access. Opening a gate allows unhampered heavenly access to an area, while closing a gate restricts access by malevolent spirits. An important detail to recall about gates is that the city gates were where financial transactions occurred in the city. The arts & entertainment mountain is an area where we definitely see warfare at the present time. New Age leaders understand the importance of gates in their respective regions and areas of influence. WISE regularly addresses and counters the New Age takeover of Hollywood, such as the time I opened a gate through prayer in downtown Hollywood above the Walk of the Stars during Halloween, 2011.

Gates in the Bible

Psalm 24:7-9 is all about gates: "Lift up your heads, you gates; be lifted up, you ancient doors, that the King of glory may come in. Who is this King of glory? The Lord strong and mighty, the Lord mighty in battle. Lift up your heads, you gates; lift them up, you ancient doors, that the King of glory may come in."

Your clients' intercessors and spiritual coaches are gate openers and territory definers. Warfare can be at the level of principalities; remember that both fallen angels and God's angels are considered principalities. God has his principalities, his archangels. Your client's enterprise can have strong, even arch-, angels assigned to it. It also can have evil principalities operating through it because of iniquity in, or curses on, the people in those organizations, regions, or territories. We are to open heavenly portals (open heaven) of revelation over our clients' organizations so that the angels have access when needed, and so they can bring the resources "down the ladder" from heaven. By the way, your clients are the ladders they descend through!

In Matthew 18:16, Jesus says for every fact to be confirmed by two or three witnesses: "But if they will not listen, take one or two others along, so that 'every matter may be established by the testimony of two or three witnesses.'" I Cor. 14:3 tells us that prophecy is given for edification, exhortation, and comfort. "But the one who prophesies speaks to people for their strengthening, encouraging and comfort."

"It is the Spirit of prophecy who bears testimony to Jesus" (Rev. 19:10b), so prophecy is the voice of Jesus. The Spirit of prophecy builds up, encourages, confirms, and brings comfort and rousing calls to change. In contrast, someone who is operating in the office of the prophet may say words that are not so comforting to people, such as words of correction, which are for their good: "And He gave some *as* apostles, and some *as* prophets, and some *as* evangelists, and some *as* pastors and teachers, *for the equipping of the saints for the work of service,* to the building up of the body of Christ ... but speaking the truth in love, we are to grow up in *all aspects* into Him who is the head, *even* Christ" (Eph. 4:11-12,15 NASB, emphasis mine). The office of the prophet is the office of one operating in a much higher level of anointing of prophecy and revelation than is seen in someone who has a prophetic mantle or someone who is operating in the simple gift of prophecy.

You are a gate opener and territory definer.

The purpose of this book is not to delve into the depths of the theology of the prophetic, but rather to emphasize that this gift is essential for ministering to your client, and it is used to discern the real battle going on in your client's life and organization.‡ There are many good books on the prophetic. I recommend Dr. Bill Hamon's excellent book *Prophets and Personal Prophecy: God's Prophetic Voice Today.*[3]

A New Finishing Anointing—Josephs Work Together

We are running in a finishing new anointing now.

You see, Joseph was a planner—not just a dreamer, not just an interpreter. He was strategic and methodical. He personally supervised the building of the storage containers so that when the famine struck, the grain was ready to fulfill the needs of the people. That supply lasted for seven years (see Gen. 41). God is doing the same thing today and many lives shall be saved, even unbelievers', through God's *new Josephs,* of which you are a part. You must be, for how can you interpret the mysteries and the dreams of your client's business team and bring them into breakthrough unless you have a new Joseph anointing? This is also combined with the Issachar anointing.

---

‡ See I Corinthians 14:5.

Favor and breakthrough — you can have them in your own life and in the lives of your clients.

Favor

If there were any areas where I could say specifically that WISE has an anointing or ability, it would be in the areas of favor and breakthrough. I would define *favor* as seeing doors open without the client having to do anything in the natural realm to cause them to open. For example, rather than favor simply showing up in the form of phone calls for orders on your new product—a product just advertised on the *Home Shopping Network*—favor would be the president of HSN saying, "We want to add the *entire line* to our upcoming shows!" Now *that* is favor.

God's favor comes out of the blue and hits you like a ton of bricks, in a good way. God's favor floors you and leaves you speechless. God's favor does not come from nothing—you either have the fruit of favor in your life (which is produced from obedience and sacrifice), or you partner with someone who has it, and voilà, things change almost immediately. For example, when someone brings WISE on board, logjams in the spirit realm become dislodged. I can't tell how many clients have said that as soon as we began to pray for them, they felt something shift. Something does shift; it's like God takes the favor on our lives and places it on your clients' enterprises. Not only that, but he *loves* to do it! Do I sound excited about the subject of favor, God's divine favor, heaven's favor? It's because *I am*.

We at WISE have this favor. You have this book in your hands, and you will benefit from this favor as well. May it be imparted to you through the reading of this book. We are nothing special in ourselves, but he calls us special and beloved. He is the only one who is begotten of the Father and worthy of all praise, because Jesus paid the price so that we could walk in the Father's favor.

Breakthrough

Breakthrough is a spiritual force, and it may even be an angel. Breakthrough is that supernatural power that overcomes an obstacle. It is very closely tied to the gift of faith—not just saving faith, but supernatural faith which can do the miraculous (see I Cor:12).

Breakthrough comes in many different forms, but some of the more common ways are through praise and worship. Ascending to such a level in warfare praise breaks through the enemy's hold over your mind, body, emotions, etc.; or someone else's mind, body, or emotions.

Breakthrough may come into a situation or circumstance by bringing a divine healing, a sudden order that was needed, or an unexpected payment.

Whatever the area of breakthrough needed, angels are certainly involved as well.

Perhaps the angel Gabriel is involved in delivering an important piece of communication you have been waiting for, or the angel Michael is involved in defeating the enemy that has been oppressing you, or perhaps a lesser angel is involved in the breakthrough. How God does it is immaterial, but the fact that he does it is the point. The fact that one minute ago something happened and I, or my situation, or my wife's situation is not the same anymore, means that a miracle happened. This is what WISE Ministries brings to the table. Things change when we come aboard; we feel the warfare immediately and go into battle, many times against a ruling spirit that is involved, and God breaks it. God's favor floors you and leaves you speechless.

We are not novices; we have been involved in many battles with territorial spirits, spirits the Bible calls rulers in high places. "For our struggle is not against flesh and blood, but against the rulers, against the authorities, against the powers of this dark world and against the spiritual forces of evil in the heavenly realms" (Eph. 6:12). Many times the battle is totally invisible and does not manifest in the natural realm; however, sometimes it manifests in the natural with signs and wonders.

Expect breakthrough as a WISE-trained coach, CP, or CRO. You may desperately need breakthrough, although you most likely could not put it into words. Breakthrough comes through Holy Spirit administrating or directing the angels, on the behalf of another toward you, through their words and bodies. They are conduits for his flowing power and administration. Their words are eternal and powerful and divinely inspired as they direct the flow of the river of God to bring that needed breakthrough to the earth realm from the heavenly realm. God even wants to do these things through you.

Experience his love and his breakthrough and his favor right now.

Enjoy it, bask in it. You are going to a new level right now; by faith claim it and receive it. Receive a new anointing.

Chapter 4: Endnotes

1. Marshall, Rich. *God@Work* and *God @ Work: Developing Ministers in the Marketplace*, Vol. 2. Shippensburg: Destiny Image Publishers, 2005.

2. Myers, Erin. "Patchwork Quilting — A History Summary" Fibre2Fashion. www.fibre2fashion.com/industry-article/ business- management-articles-reports/patchwork-quilting-a-history-summary/ patchwork-quilting-a-history-summary1.asp

3. Hamon, Bill, and Oral Roberts. *Prophets and Personal Prophecy: God's Prophetic Voice Today*. Shippensburg: Destiny Image, 2011.

Recommended Additional Resources for Leaders

Books

Hillman, Os. *The 9-5 Window: How Faith Can Transform the Workplace*

DVDs/CDs/MP3s

Hillman, Os. "How We Lost the 7 Mountains" MP3, www.tgifbookstore.com

People

Rich Marshall, ROI | godisworking.com

C. Peter Wagner, Wagner Leadership Institute
www.wagnerleadership.org

Charging for Services

"I have been using the services of WISE Ministries for the last three months and have found it to be a tremendous blessing. The team has been very supportive of me, and my coach was great. She always had an encouraging word to say and many words of wisdom.

The prayers and support I received really helped me, and I know that the Lord was answering those prayers and healing me of various issues and challenges I was facing. It was great to know that I had a team of committed people supporting me through some very difficult times.

I wouldn't hesitate to recommend WISE to anyone."

— Natalie B., Darby, England

5

"Now to the one who works, wages are not credited as a gift but as an obligation" (Romans 4:4).

"The worker deserves his wages" (Luke 10:7b).

Your Spiritual Advisory Team Is Paid to Solve Problems

The ultimate breakthroughs all belong to God. Your SAT moves in his power, his revelation, and his grace. Jesus said "I no longer call you servants, because a servant does not know his master's business. Instead, I have called you friends, for everything that I learned from my Father I have made known to you" (John 15:5). God will make you look good through your SAT. Remember that. You look good when you simply work alongside your SAT and are obedient in relating and, in some cases interpreting, revelation.

Obedience is the currency of heaven. Jesus said, "If you love me, keep my commands" (John 14:15). Obedience is equivalent to love in the Bible. If you are obedient, you will be successful in solving problems for your client's organization. Solving problems entails getting to the root of those problems. There are many different types of problems which need solving—financial, marital, personnel, operational—or controlling spirits, confusion in the marketing and message, etc. Sometimes the problems have to do with the leadership

and those whom your client has hired. As I said before, your allegiance must be to the Lord, who is your ultimate source. He will help you to urge and coax your clients, in love, to change.

> "Therefore, I urge you, brothers and sisters, in view of God's mercy, to offer your bodies as a living sacrifice, holy and pleasing to God—this is your true and proper worship. Do not conform to the pattern of this world, but be transformed by the renewing of your mind. Then you will be able to test and approve what God's will is—his good, pleasing and perfect will" (Rom. 12:1-2).

He has called you to your line of work. "Being confident of this, that he who began a good work in you will carry it on to completion until the day of Christ Jesus" (Phil. 1:6).

Your client is the leader and the chief spiritual officer (CSO), and has the ultimate say (and responsibility) when dealing with the spiritual matters of her organization. She can dedicate or rededicate her organization to the Lord, even right now.

The Lord Jesus is the CEO, but she is also the CEO—Christ's Equipped Officer.

You Charge for Christian Coaching? New Times Demand New Methods

I need to rephrase the question. You charge for your coaching time? The answer is YES. The coaching is offered up freely but the time is not. In other words, your time spent coaching is valuable and, as such, you should be compensated for the time spent in ministering to your client's various needs. Of course we charge for coaching.

One major purpose of this book is to validate and verify that the need for certification in the coaching field is both for professionalism and for accountability, and to give you that credibility.

Professionalism
- through certification (the purpose of this class)
- through standards
- through belonging to the IAMC (International Association of Marketplace Coaches) or a similar network

Accountability
- through relationships and regular reporting or checking in
  » with the CROs or CEOs
  » with clients — via e-mail updates and/or sessions with their business team, and possibly their spouses
  » with others on their spiritual advisory teams
- through the production of reports that come out of the intercession times with God
- through recorded, regular coaching sessions with them that you have forwarded to their PLIs

In addition, there is a feedback loop in which clients can give the coach and intercessor updates as to which things to stop addressing, along with new updates.

Say you are a pastor. Do you charge your congregation for each sermon that you preach? That would be absurd. Your congregation supports you for your time and the value of your ministry. So think of yourself as your clients' supporter in the ministry to which God has called them and for which he has gifted them; your clients are paying for your time, the fruit of your relationship with God, and your giftedness.

We don't pay our pastors just to preach a sermon; their ministry is much more expansive than that, and so is the ministry of the PLI, the SC, and the CP. It's so much more than advice or prayer; it's spiritual discernment, confirmation, encouragement, and recording (prayer and coaching sessions) what God is saying. It's warfare against the spiritual forces that are coming against your client and his enterprise. It's devising strategies to defend against and prevent spiritual attacks. It's going ahead of the enemy in the Spirit. Too long have we relegated spiritual ministry to being free and not dared charge for it.

My well thought-out and rehearsed answer to questions goes like this: "Well, you pay a professional pastor, you pay a professional missionary, so why not pay a spiritual advisory team? Are they not as important to God as a pastor?" Wait; come to think of it, don't ask that! *Keep in mind that your clients are not only paying for spiritual services, they are also covering our operational costs, management costs, hiring costs, etc.*

The truth is all these people *are* just as important, and so is the machinist, the janitor, and the CEO too! Our work is our ministry, period. We don't differ in importance to God, just in our function. The word "work" in Greek, the language of the New Testament, comes from the root word *avodah,* which is the same root word as for the Greek word for worship. We worship in church, and we worship in work and *through* our work.

I am writing this to bring these intercessors, coaches, and prophets into the twenty-first century ministry and to combine their giftings (in business, art, education, or government) along with the spiritual gifts to complete the kingdom company model.

Seven mountain coaches are like the hidden treasure

"For Scripture says, 'Do not muzzle an ox while it is treading out the grain,' and 'The worker deserves his wages'" (I Tim. 5:18).

"We always thank God for all of you and continually mention you in our prayers" (I Thess. 1:2).

"And the people came to Moses and said, 'We have sinned, for we have spoken against the Lord and against you. Pray to the Lord, that he take away the serpents from us.' So Moses prayed for the people" (Num. 21:7 ESV).

"The kingdom of heaven is like treasure hidden in a field. When a man found it, he hid it again, and then in his joy went and sold all he had and bought that field" (Matt. 13:44).

Holy Spirit spoke to me, saying that those who operate in spiritual services are like the treasure buried in the field or assigned to *your client's field*—that is in *your client's* field of ministry, whether it is business, art, education, etc. When your client finds his coach, it is like his finding of buried treasure. He will do anything for her because he knows her prophetic voice and encouragement is the *key* to his breakthrough.

You have been hidden just for your clients, and you are *tied to their land,* that is, you have the authority! If you do not know about their land (field) you will learn, but God has already given you that land.

You are the specialist they need. Do not let your giftedness remain buried any longer.

Be sure to have your client train you about his organization and be sure to meet his senior leaders with the SAT's PLI. [The minimum recommended WISE SAT configuration is an SC and at least one PLI. Many times there are also CPs, the CRO, and multiples PLIs.] Complete an onsite assessment. (If you are taking the certification class, you will be given a sample assessment.)

Your client's SAT members are a treasure hidden in darkness. "I will give you hidden treasures, riches stored in secret places, so that you may know that I am the Lord, the God of Israel, who summons you by name" (Isa. 45:3). Only when you are found can your light shine forth. "Arise, shine, for your light has come, and the glory of the Lord rises upon you" (Isa. 60:1).

Money Is spiritual

You have to be good with your finances—good with God (not under condemnation), as well as good with the concept of being paid for your services and that you are worth what you charge. Second, you will need to convince or encourage your decision makers that spiritual services are worth being paid for.

> *"Give the first and the best to sanctify the whole and the rest."*
>
> — Robert Henderson,
> *The Caused Blessing*

God loves a cheerful (hilarious) giver.

Whatever we do, we "work at it with all [our] heart, as working for the Lord, not for human masters" (Col. 3:23). We give to man in the frame of acting as a channel to God.

God's promise of prosperity

Prosperity is not just financial success. Prosperity has within it the meaning of success at all levels in life: physical, emotional, mental, spiritual, etc. I am prosperous if I am doing the will of God and if there is peace in my marriage and family. As coaches, our job is to seek prosperity the way God has defined it for ourselves, our fellow coaches, our clients, and our families.

A poverty spirit

A poverty spirit or mentality is a state of mind where money is always an issue. How do I know if I have a poverty spirit?

> *Do you find yourself thinking about money frequently?*

- Do you know that people who are wealthy can have a poverty mentality? If they are almost obsessed with their money, then the answer is yes, they have a poverty spirit.

- How do I get free from the poverty spirit?

Books have been written on this subject. One of the main solutions is to live below your means. This way you are not always pressed to come up with money.

> "Most people do not see prosperity in their lives because they do not expect to prosper! ... What we expect from life is often a direct result of our desires, whether they are Holy Spirit-prompted or not ... This is a time to break out of the shell of your last identity, whether good or bad. God is doing a new thing with his people and creating a new model of kingdom authority in the earth. You are a part of this! It is time to break the spirit of poverty from your life. Poverty thinking is contrary to faith, and without faith you cannot please God. You please God when you have a mind to prosper."
>
> — Chuck D. Pierce & Robert Heidler[1]

Prosperity is not just financial success. Prosperity has within it the meaning of success at all levels in life: physical, emotional, mental, spiritual, etc. I am prosperous if I am doing the will of God and if there is peace in my marriage and family. As coaches, our job is to seek prosperity the way God has defined it for ourselves, our fellow leaders, our clients, and our families.

Why Should a CEO Compensate You for This Ministry?
WISE uses the firstfruits model as outlined in Scripture

Once we give God our first and our best, he will take, bless, and multiply that which remains. We ask that our clients pay us for the month in advance as a firstfruit offering unto the Lord.

Remember, tell your clients to pay the SAT team first. Just be up front, and be confident in your value and worth to your client.

- This is part of the reward for the coaches and intercessors, and it is given into the apostolic ministry. The apostolic ministry has the ability to fully reproduce its DNA. Scripture says that there are different levels of rewards or multiplication—some thirty, sixty, and hundredfold (see Matthew 13:23). The soil is important, and it is what produces the increase. The apostolic soil is the most productive. Not all ministries produce the same fruit, and God is calling on us to examine those ministries and to listen to God's voice as to where to give. Your clients' WISE SAT members are good ground.
- Remember, apostles bring breakthrough. Apostolic ministry has the ability to remove mountains, because it is largely assisted by the angelic realm and carries with it the authority of heaven (to make decrees). The apostolic ministry is preceded by meekness—power under control. Moses was a type of apostle, and he was the meekest man on the face of the earth (see Numbers 12:3).

> "Modern-day Levites are pastors and modern-day priests are apostles."
>
> — Robert Henderson, *The Caused Blessing*

- This is an ongoing relationship; your client is not paying for an answer or a breakthrough, but is supporting a relationship. Again, relationships are paramount. God wants to support your clients, but they must have wisdom. They must desire the best for their SATs and love them, protect them, and pastor them. Then they will want to provide for you because the two of you are in covenant—many times for life.
- PLIs and SCs are on a par with church-paid ministerial staff. The purpose of this book is to update and inform coaches that there

are CEOs and other seven mountain leaders that need a professional, certified level of spiritual expertise and involvement within all seven mountains of culture. These trained personnel can operate in the local church, Hollywood, government, education, etc. in order to bless it.

The main point here is about honor and expertise in making things happen for you and your client's enterprise. This is a level of proficiency that deserves financial compensation and recognition similar to that of other church staff and professional positions. For too long, the spiritual service experts have hidden out in the church. Now God is calling them into the light, and to—as the apostle Paul said to Timothy his son—"discharge all the duties of your ministry" (II Tim. 4:5).

In our WISE model, intercessors and coaches are like Peter out fishing for a breakthrough, answer, or direction from God. Peter was a professional fisherman and usually fished with nets, not a hook. The hook speaks of accuracy and specificity—the kind of prophetic guidance your client needs. One fish and one hook; let's connect you … God has a problem in your client's life with his WISE team's name on it. The problem is being used to get his attention so he can connect with WISE to get to where he needs to be.

God allows the problems in people's lives for a reason. Your client may not have a business problem, but rather a marriage problem that God wants to work on. God can have a hook in us—his sons and daughters—and he may need to work on a specific issue; that is why he is allowing your client to experience what he is going through. I promise he is being redemptive in allowing this, and your client's end result will be better than his beginning. In another sense, *your coach* is the fish with the coin in *his* mouth—the coin that solves *your* problem too.

We all have problems or needs, and God is keenly aware of them. Every coach needs a coach, every intercessor needs an intercessor, and every leader needs both! These relationships are always a win-win.

SAT members are on the frontlines of the spiritual battle, and as such, need prayer cover. As intercessors and coaches, we see the need to have professional intercessors praying for us and mentors to coach us; however, we encourage our clients to also pray for us and advise us. When they do, it is a blessing for them too. We do not let them totally outsource spiritual ministry, because they will be robbed of a blessing if they do. We pray reciprocally for them, and vice versa, because we are family. As you will see, I do not shy away from being amply rewarded for my efforts, because many times what we do is the *key* to their breakthrough. It's a win-win relationship.

> *We establish a baseline and a benchmark that recognizes and rewards those trained.*

The fact that this industry can be very prosperous comes with a price that must be paid in spiritual warfare, humility, travel requirements to our clients' sites, and the accompanying physical wear and tear on our bodies. For those of you who have been in spiritual warfare, you know it can be grueling at times. Your travel needs will be dictated by whether you are both coach and intercessor or fill one role, and by how large your client's enterprise is, what his immediate needs are, and how many leaders in his organization need ministry. As his SAT stands in the gap for him, his enterprises, family, and territories, he will see great breakthroughs. Any pain endured to see real change will be worth it, and you will be handsomely rewarded.

God is waiting to bless your client. What is needed is for you to walk into your client's life. You are like a key to a door that has been locked. God just places the key (you) in the lock and turns it to open the door.

> In the certification course, I show you how to negotiate by giving a mock demonstration. As we talk about the skeptical client, we also cover how to overcome objections.

Why Do We Charge for WISE's Services?

We have, in the past and also currently, given free services to many clients for many months ... our reason being that we feel the Lord is telling us to do so, and/or we want potential clients to see the value of our services, and/or some cannot afford to pay for services at the time, yet they really need ministry, etc. Why not always give it away? That is *the* question many have in their minds. It originates with people being confused about the *value* of spiritual ministry and the separation of church, business, and the other five mountains. Which mountain supports spiritual ministry—the church or business?

We, as good church members, have focused on giving to God with our tithes and not on funding the pastoral staff or the church mortgage—this has been good for church leadership, but not so good for us. We don't associate that 5 percent of our tithe just went toward the preaching of a sermon or toward having the lights on for the Sunday morning service. There has been a lack of specificity regarding *where* our money goes. For example, when I was young I gave thousands of dollars to a well-publicized ministry. Did my money go for winning souls or for a fountain in the new building? *I don't know.* Our giving as Christians can sometimes seem to go into a black hole.

As a result, good church people are used to giving but not to paying for specific, spiritually oriented services. Counseling is the exception, but that's not WISE's main ministry (even though counseling is a component of what we do when we coach our clients).

WISE exists to be an extension of the church for our businesspeople and leaders in all of the seven mountains. Businesspeople are used to being the ones who write the checks and solve the problems in a church. Is the extent of their ministry ushering or receiving the offering? Quite frankly, they are used to being prostituted; many pastors see their businesspeople as being provision for their own visions. Businesspeople are not generally honored in the church. Our number one goal as WISE coaches is to honor and encourage our people.

Honor

> *WISE is about relationship and honor. How do you place a price tag on honor? This is the challenge.*

Our clients need to *know* that they have been placed with their SATs by God for mutual benefit, and that they need you in order to reach their destinies in God—not just in business, relationships, or finances, but in their *destinies*. Issachar speaks to this; tribe members honored and cared for their brothers and sisters in the other tribes. They lived to see the other tribes become successful and would fight anyone who stood in the way. Your clients need you to recognize and awaken their potential and calling in God.

This *cannot* be overstated. We have seen our clients grow and blossom into mighty men and women of God over the years. It's *your* time to do the same for your clients! It is a new day; welcome to marketplace ministry (and ministry in all spheres, not just in the church).

Chapter 5: Endnotes

1. Pierce, Chuck D. and Robert Heidler. *A Time to Prosper, Finding and Entering God's Realm of Blessings.* Ventura: Regal, 2013.

Recommended Additional Resources for Coaches

Books

> C. Peter Wagner, *Prayer Shield: How to Intercede for Pastors, Christian Leaders and Others on the Spiritual Frontlines* (Prayer Warrior Series)
>
> Robert Henderson, *The Caused Blessing: Connecting to Apostolic Power Through Strategic Giving*
>
> Bill Hamon, *Prophetic Scriptures Yet to Be Fulfilled: During the 3rd and Final Reformation*

DVDs/CDs

> Randy DeMain's sermons on the Sons of Issachar
> www.kingdomrevelation.org

People

> Robert Henderson, Robert Henderson Ministries
> www.roberthenderson.org
>
> Randy Demain, Kingdom Revelation Mnistries
> www.kingdomrevelation.org
>
> Bill Hamon, Christian International Ministries Network
> www.christianinternational.com

Coaching Leaders

"Pastor Charles prayed prophetically over my wife and me in February 2009. Among many personal words of the Lord that were received and clarified throughout the year, there was a word given about our investment business, Kingdom Legacy Fund. The Lord spoke through Charles and indicated the fund would have returns of over 100 percent, and even up to 800 percent coming. I must admit, my mind didn't really grasp those levels of returns as our best year was 18 percent, and the worst ever was just over 12 percent; we considered those to be good enough for anyone.

As I prepared for strategic planning for 2010 by just doing some number crunching, I calculated that we had increased capital to invest by 846 percent, and the annual return for 2009 was 100 percent better than our best year—18 percent in 2002 to 36 percent in 2009. The numbers didn't translate in my mind as earnings, but they did translate into impact for our company and for our clients. We are grateful to WISE for its continued prayer for our business, clients, and principals of Kingdom Legacy Fund."

— John M., Fort Lauderdale, FL

6

"Not by might nor by power, but by my Spirit, says the Lord Almighty" (Zechariah 4:6b).

Ministering to Leaders and Their Unique Needs*

You have unique responsibilities and pressures ministering to leaders running an enterprise (such as a business). Things happen. They have to stay on top of every obstacle that comes their way—meet payroll during difficult times or shortfalls, deal with an IRS audit, cover the loss of two leaders who give their notices at the same time, attend to a lawsuit—all within the space of a few days. WISE-certified spiritual, life, and executive coaches are aware of this, because many of our personnel have owned and operated organizations themselves.

We all need someone to give us permission to be whom God has called us to be.

We understand our clients' pain in this highly competitive global marketplace, and we ask the Lord for a Romans 12:15 "rejoice with those who rejoice and weep with those who weep" baptism and identification with these seven mountain leaders. Until we identify with our clients and their leaders, the Lord may not give us glimpses into their hearts and struggles—an essential before we can weep between the porch and the altar as a modern-day priest for them.

"Let the priests, who minister before the Lord, weep between the portico and the altar. Let them say, 'Spare your people, Lord. Do not make your inheritance an object of scorn, a byword among the nations. Why should they say among the peoples, "Where is their God?"'" (Joel 2:17).

---

* For some of the specific areas we can pray for you, see C. Peter Wagner's book, *Prayer Shield: How to Intercede for Pastors, Christian Leaders and Others on the Spiritual Frontlines* (Prayer Warrior Series)

Clients seeking spiritual support for their enterprise(s) may have many questions they want answered.

> How can I know that my business or enterprise has the favor of God?
>
> Can we receive the results that we would like?
>
> Will doors be opened to new business without us having to do it via our own efforts?
>
> Can families of leaders be at peace? Can employees be at peace with each other?
>
> Will financial doors be opened?
>
> Will God still prosper us in the midst of attacks—whether verbal, gossip, slander…?
>
> Is the enemy resisting us, yet unable to stop us?
>
> Is our faith being tested?
>
> Does God care about my enterprise? Can God be involved with my enterprise above and beyond just blessing it in some general amorphous sense?
>
> What hidden dangers exist if I am passive in my Christian walk toward my enterprise?
>
> What if there are hindrances that I am unaware of? Can my enterprise be healed and set free from these hindrances?
>
> I feel like I am walking the tightrope right now. What can I do?
>
> What part do I play in the success or failure of the enterprise as its leader?
>
> How can my enterprise be a powerful tool in the hands of the Lord in its own right?
>
> I am not sure that I can continue if things do not change. Is there help?
>
> *The answer is YES! Let us help you in the way we have helped hundreds of others. There is hope!*

Relationship → Destiny

Spiritual, life, and executive coaches get this. What we do is about the connection with our client, which then leads to a relationship, which then leads to him becoming all that God has ordained for him. You as a coach are an enabler of this.

> As a coach, you have a stage and a platform to speak into your clients' lives and situations. They are open and they want to improve. Sock it to them! Wow them with the awesome simplicity and straightforwardness of the power of God and his gifts operating through you. You have been waiting your whole life to get to this level of wisdom and ministry. You may be the only person that they can talk with about certain things. This is a coveted and honorable position that God has given you in their lives. Cherish this. Only someone called to be a coach will understand what I am saying. I never take it for granted.

Additionally, I only certify people that I feel have the gifting and temperament to be a coach from the beginning. You cannot have someone learn to be a coach; you can fine-tune him or her, but you cannot place something inside of him that God has not put there from the beginning. Does that make sense? [You have read this far, so you probably have the gift.]

What Is a Destiny Link?

We are all born with innate spiritual strengths and weaknesses. We come into this world needing each other. We grow in life needing each other. At WISE, we call our need for others *destiny links*.[†] Types of destiny links include:

- someone sent by God to get you to your next assignment, or
- a seasoned advisor who has already been where you are going, e.g., Jonathan and David, Elijah and Elisha, Paul and Barnabas

Each Enterprise Is a Spiritual Entity and Has a Destiny

An enterprise, whether profit or nonprofit, is a spiritual entity. It has a spiritual destiny to fulfill. We are creators, like our Father.

---

† A term coined by Sandie Freed in her book *Destiny Thieves*

Organizations provide provision and sustenance for the owners and employees, but they also have a *social responsibility* to their regions and are to be giving centers. We believe that every organization needs to give a percentage off the top to worthy causes. This and other attributes are ascribed to *kingdom companies*.‡

When God places a creative spark inside a company's founder, it is because he has a *life* purpose for the company to fulfill—a spiritual blueprint which encapsulates its destiny. This destiny may be unfolding; it may not be known in its entirety early on.

When God saved and called you, he put a destiny and a blueprint inside you with detailed instructions on what he has called you to do on the earth. One of these outworks is your client's enterprise(s). (I don't just call it a business, because we could be talking about a studio, political office, family, classroom, TV or radio station, church, etc. Each one of these examples is a part of God's—now man's—creation, and is a part of the kingdom of God if it has been properly dedicated and commissioned by God.)

In the 2013 Tipping Point Annual Unconference, we awarded our Social Transformation Company of the Year Award to the Atlanta, Georgia-based CKS Packaging.§ CKS gave 2.8 million dollars from their top line to over forty-eight ministries in 2012. They feed and clothe and help prepare literally thousands of children and adults for school by distributing backpacks and supplies to through their Maximum Impact Love ministry,¶ which is on company grounds. They directly impact the neighborhoods in which they work.

The Importance of Motives

Why are our clients seeking coaching? What do they want to get out of it?

We are looking for motives here. Motives matter; if their motive is to increase profits, that's okay just as long as they are willing for God to address any necessary issues related to achieving that result—in the company and in their personal lives and marriages. Rarely will the typical client list this, by the way. It is like dating. You and your potential client will be on your best behaviors. No one wants

---

‡ For more on kingdom companies, see my 2 DVD set "Taking Your Company to the Next Level Spiritually," which is available from our WISE online store at the link "WISE Online Store Links for DVDs" on page 112, and which will be provided to each student in the certification course.
§ www.ckspackaging.com
¶ www.ckspackaging.com/our-company/social-responsibility/maximum-impact-love/

to appear greedy. You will quote your client a fair amount for the spiritual services he needs.[1] Sometimes God gets the attention of leaders by touching the revenue stream.

> *Once the root problems are solved and issues addressed, the revenue might suddenly jump.*

If the motive of a client is pure greed and/or he has an idol of mammon, the Lord will reveal this to us and we may not be released to take him on as a client. If he is not truly saved but desires ministry, that will not work either. This ministry is for saved and fairly mature leaders of enterprises.

Contract versus covenant

The world understands contracts. If one party fails to uphold the contract, he pays a price.

Covenant is God's way to do things. It is God who ultimately upholds his part of the covenant by providing results, and we are not bogged down by dishonorable people.

> *While there is a contract between you and your SAT, the basis of that covenant is that God is the third person involved.*

> *God takes a contract very seriously. The seven mountains require and expect professionalism, so contracts are vital. They reflect the earthly reality of a spiritual commitment.*

Money is spiritual. "For where your treasure is, there your heart will be also." (Matt. 6:21)

The seven mountains require and expect professionalism, so contracts are vital. They reflect the earthly reality of a spiritual committment. God upholds his side of the contract through his representatives—his intercessors, coaches, and marketplace pastors.

When we have a contract in which finances are exchanged for services, this legal document creates *the reality* (builds a structure in the Spirit realm) of what we are trying to achieve. God *honors and upholds* the content of the contract.

God takes contracts (covenants) very seriously. This is the *missing ingredient* for those who do not value the services rendered and are not willing to pay for them. Numerous clients have begun to see positive results (financial, emotional, relational) soon after signing the contract—they see logjams being removed in the Spirit when they align with their professional SAT and WISE. It's like your client has been waiting forever for her strategic intelligence team to come along and to *apostolically align* or unlock her organization and life. *Now* is the day of salvation for her life, family, and organization.

The law of intention or intentionality: Leaders draw those resources to themselves when they make a conscious intent in their hearts to produce a certain result and to walk in a certain direction.

During a Typical Coaching Session

In some cases, your client may not know that you are a Christian, but you probably have books and posters in your office that make it obvious that you are a believer. If you are on Skype, you are in control of what your client sees in the background.

WISE coaches frequently do inner healing, deliverance, and counseling, but make sure your client knows that you are not a licensed counselor (if that is the case). In some cases you will not have the necessary knowledge and experience, in which case, you can refer her to an inner healing specialist for that issue and move onto an area that you do feel comfortable with. WISE spiritual and life coaches are healers, and the more tools we have on our belts, the better. You may not see yourself as a healer right now, but you will work into it.

Show empathy, love, and respect. Never hurry the session along to reach your goals, as can be the case with many professional coaches and counselors. You're here, in this place and time, for her. Emotional healing is slower than spiritual healing, in most cases. Let your client cry as much as she wants. This may be the first time in a long time she has felt safe enough to do so. Be patient and listen. Comfort her verbally. [Always keep the door opened at least a crack and, preferably, have a window in your coaching office. We want to always avoid the appearance of sin.]

Begin, or continue work, on an area in your client's personal and/or spiritual life, work situation, ministry planning, etc. If you work on a marital issue, (you may have both spouses in your office or on Skype for this). Most of my sessions are over Skype or some other visual mechanism. I highly recommend that you do audio and video, not just audio.

Be ready for Holy Spirit to show up at any point in the session. He is in charge of the session and is the master coach and counselor. He makes your job much easier when you follow his leading.

Goal Setting and Milestones

Goal setting is very important, especially for businesses, in the beginning of the fiscal year. Our coaches and client leaders get together for a day or two to plan the entire year's goals—financial, output, employees. We lay them before the Lord and they are almost *always* met or exceeded. The companies that do not do this may see increase during the year, thanks to the coaching and intercession, but the increase is not as much (compared to those who have set goals).

Intercession requires specificity in prayer, and God is gracious to meet or exceed those results when the leadership team is listening to and obeying God. Personal goals for your life and spiritual coaching clients are also very important.

Milestones relate to interim benchmarks during the coaching process or quarterly reviews for an organization. When you set out yearly goals with your clients, encourage them to then place the goals into quarterly segments so as to spur them on.

TOOLS TO HELP YOUR CLIENT (AND YOU) BUILD A GODLY BUSINESS

- The Word
- The Spirit[1]
- Prayer and coaching – implementing an SAT
- A heart for the lost – especially in your client's organization
- A mission statement that includes the Lord
- A vision statement that includes God's calling
- A kingdom giving plan
- A commitment to personal growth and development on the part of the leader(s)
- Inviting God in subtle ways into the HR manual – including godly practices.

We do not need full unity when implementing these tools, just agreement with at least one of the major leaders on board.

Coaching Well

In any of these modalities, you first need to:

Be comfortable with yourself and your place in life. Are you a truly happy person? Are you happy being a seven mountains professional coach? If not, this will come through to your client. Your client definitely needs to feel better after your session. That is not to say that he won't be emotionally exhausted or thoroughly challenged, depending upon what was covered in the session. Sometimes he may even leave with his tail between his legs because of a swift kick in the pants you gave him (in love, of course). The peace from your self-confident identity will exude from you.

You are coaching because you like it and have overcome some or most of the same obstacles that your client is now going through. You have it within you to develop a roadmap for your client's success. God will help you. This is why it is important to offer a package of services for a defined length of time. Do not sell yourself or your abilities short, or limit the package to a short period, because you are worth it.

You are a winner, a success.

Not unlike a counselor, your mere presence brings peace, comfort, understanding, and clarity to your client. It is who you are that shows up in the session. You do not have to strive to be who you are, you just are!

Do you love to coach? Your clients will be helped out of their ruts, their bondages, their self-defeating thinking, and subsequent negative behaviors. You are so very important to their lives. You are a professional coach and people are paying you for your life and leadership or organizational experience. They want you! In reality they want to be like you. Don't ever forget that.

Know that the tools you employ will help a lot, bring variety, and give a more complete picture. You are not alone; you have this guide, possibly the certification class, and access to WISE Ministries for advice and all of our tools.

Do not compare yourself to other coaches; that is a trap. Coaches love to talk themselves up. When you compare yourself to others, the one we compare ourselves to is almost always better anyway, and that is why this is a trap. I encourage you to develop your own signature tools and aids for your clients, such as visual aids or charts. It will help reinforce what you deeply believe and what has worked for you.

A prayer: *Lord, help us all to discern the signs of the times, but also to be diligent—with the gifts and connections you have given to each of us and in the fulfillment of our callings.*

Hiring an SAT member as an employee or a consultant?

There are many advantages and disadvantages to consider when a coach is an employee vs. consultant. As with a garden, the CEO can either plant her own seeds or import some seeds (consultants). Either way, she is growing her own expertise akin to growing her own food supply (vegetables), which can be used to provide sustenance during a time of famine and even save lives. Whether your client chooses WISE to supply intercessors, coaches, and other advisory team members, or she decides to hire her own consultant, know that lives will be saved and enhanced by the wisdom, spiritual, business, and organizational aptitudes that our coaches possess.

Your SAT's effects could include the protection and strengthening of marriages and families; the fulfillment of spiritual destiny in personal, financial, business, and ministry areas; and the avoidance of heartbreaking missteps.

The One

As a coach, remember that you are still called to the one.

Jesus, the Shepherd, left the ninety-nine sheep to find the one that was lost and carried him back on his shoulders (at least, that is what the painting depicts). It is an honor to be called to the one—the one you get breakthrough for, the one you coach into an entire level of new thinking or existence, the one you help to find purpose, the one you help heal or bring deliverance to.

I have seen so many wonderful breakthroughs down through the years with clients, thanks to the precious movement of Holy Spirit. God has rewarded me so highly because I forsook the ninety-nine; I forsook the crowds to heal this one—this precious one that God called me into relationship with. Now that I have spent over 2200 coaching/counseling hours (as of this writing) with many different *ones*, God has opened the door for me to write these volumes. Now many can be trained to do what *the one* (me) has done for all these years in the way God has ordained me to teach it. WISE Ministries and the Tipping Point are movements of God in the earth.

You get to be a part of it.

Liz and I and our team have climbed the moutains of our callings, if you will, and as we reach the apex, we can help you get to where you need to be too, and take this to the world.

Chapter 6: Endnotes

1. Intercessory Tools taught by Elizabeth Alves and team leaders. "Intercessory Training." Intercessors International, 2005.

Recommended Additional Resources for Readers and Students

Books

Hamon, Bill. *The Day of the Saints: Equipping Believers for Their Revolutionary Role in Ministry*

Freed, Sandie. *Destiny Thieves*

Sheets, Dutch. *History Makers: Your Prayers Have The Power To Heal The Past And Shape The Future*

Goll, Jim. *The Lost Art of Intercession: Restoring the Power and Passion of the Watch of the Lord*

DVDs/CDs

Pierce, Chuck, Robert Heidler, Linda Heidler, Paul Wilbur and Chris Hayward, "Positioned for Advancement: Understanding the Tribes and Months." www.gloryofzion.org/webstore

Os Hillman, "Reclaiming the 7 Mountains of Culture Introduction." www.tgifbookstore.com

People

Chuck Pierce, Glory of Zion International
www.gloryofzion.org

Anthony Hulsebus, Dominion Ministries
www.dominionministries.net

Bishop Bill Hamon, Christian International
www.ChristianInternational.com

Groups

Christian Business Network
www.christianbusinessnetwork.org

Elizabeth Alves, Intercessors International
www.increaseinternational.com

A 7M-Enabled Coach

"I've only been with WISE for three months, but already see benefits. Prayers that I'd been praying for quite some time have been answered on the fast track. God is doing the work, but I believe he is pleased when his children partner together to come before him. I also appreciate WISE's interest in my family, as family issues can affect business. WISE's weekly counsel has been inspiring and thought provoking. If you're unsure as to whether to partner with WISE for prayer and support ... go ahead and take the risk...God honors our faith."

— Anonymous

7

"You will also decree a thing, and it will be established for you; and light will shine on your ways" (Job 22:28 NASB).

Using Strategic Intelligence

Before I discuss strategic intelligence, I want to talk about spiritual intelligence. We have heard of other intelligences, such as emotional intelligence. It's so important, we have it in our tagline.

Spiritual intelligence is the ability to ask and to know which spiritual forces and/or dynamics are in operation.

Spiritual intelligence also helps one know how to react and respond in a variety of situations, especially in professional situations.

For example, say you (the lead spiritual coach) are invited to a company board meeting. Spiritual intelligence is knowing when to speak and what to speak, given the varied audience of C-level people—CEO, CFO, CIO, etc.—as well as board members, who may not be known as well. As a rule, you should always be ready to respond when asked a question, or when asked for your perception or discernment on an issue, and take good notes. The CEO or chairman was willing to take a risk in inviting you to the meeting, so we instruct our SAT trainees to be discrete and say few words, especially initially, and know their audiences. Being consistently involved at the board level is one of the highest honors in the spiritual services industry.

Strategic intelligence, for our purposes, carries with it all the ideas above, but it additionally has a *strategy* or *stratagems* for both the enterprises and for each individual product, service, or project the enterprises are engaged with.

Signs of the need for spiritual intelligence

Your clients may be considering coaching because they feel as if something is lacking, but they cannot quite identify what is missing. Some possible explanations are:

They have tried everything else and still find themselves lacking.

They wonder why some of their prayers, or the prayers of their intercessors, haven't been answered.

They have achieved a level of success in their enterprises, but wonder why they haven't gone to the next level.

They wonder why it seems as if they are caught up in the world's way of doing things and can't break free.

They lack a detailed roadmap of where God wants to take them and their ventures.

No one has been running interference for them and deflecting the attacks of the enemy.

No one has given them the spiritual intelligence they need.

They don't have a team that can listen to the chatter through advanced spiritual intelligence, such as the sample story in II Kings 6:8:

> "Now the king of Aram was at war with Israel. After conferring with his officers, he said, 'I will set up my camp in such and such a place.' The man of God sent word to the king of Israel: 'Beware of passing that place, because the Arameans are going down there.' So the king of Israel checked on the place indicated by the man of God. Time and again Elisha warned the king, so that he was on his guard in such places. This enraged the king of Aram. He summoned his officers and demanded of them, 'Tell me! Which of us is on the side of the king of Israel?' 'None of us, my lord the king,' said one of his officers, 'but Elisha, the prophet who is in Israel, tells the king of Israel the very words you speak in your bedroom.'"

They don't have a ministry team which immerses itself into the DNA of the client and company, one that seeks the Lord to understand the times and the seasons of their enterprise's impact through its products and services.

> See my DVD teaching, "Opening Global Gates of Access and Provision," for more on portals or gates of God. Certification students receive this DVD; others may order it via the store link on page 112.

The Importance of Your Client's Enterprise

God is "into" networks, and as such, your client's business(es), ministry, studio, governmental office, school, etc. can become a part of the regional, national, and international network of heaven. The fact that your client's enterprise resides on land and in buildings is hugely important. God wants to use his property as a beachhead to minister to his region! He wants to use it as a regional apostolic hub.

There is authority in financing, manufacturing, and ministering to people. What a powerful tool is your client's enterprise in the hand of God! If your client and his leadership are teachable and pliable, there is nothing God cannot do through the physical aspects of his company—it becomes a natural extension of heaven's spiritual effects. Again, it's all about the land. Every establishment can be an armament for the kingdom and part of the heavenly network—a launching point, which is just as important as the local church (but which differs in function) for God's angels to the territory and the region. Does this not excite you? It excites me! Put another way, God wants to use your clients' lands and buildings for his purposes. It's all part of his heavenly strategy.

Spiritual blueprint

Strategic intelligence enables you to create a plan for success in the competitive marketplace of your client's company in the areas of marketing, sales, new initiatives, etc. This level of involvement is usually made at the CRO or spiritual coach level.

Battle plan

A plan that the spiritual coach or intercessor will have some involvement with is a battle plan. This is a strategic plan that addresses the issues and resistance both within and without (outside) the company and will be a deliverable from the initial assessment (forms provided in certification class), if it was conducted. It's an onsite visit that includes interviews with key leaders, a tour of the facilities, listening (for spiritual chatter) in the offices, and other aids. The assessment helps to diagnose where the company has been and where God wants to take it.

The battle plan is a strategic intelligence plan that addresses all resistance, territorial spirits, competitors, and issues that have to be overcome. The battle plan is a forward-looking document that consists of strategies and tactics in advancing the kingdom of God through the outworking of the enterprise.

Strategic intelligence has to do with how to respond to the plethora of spiritual, management, tactical, personnel, financial, and operational issues which can arise. Remember, every issue that the company faces has a spiritual component to it. Strategic intelligence has to do with what is really going on, not just the superficial symptoms, and how to respond to it. Again, this means getting to the root of things. Consider a doctor in the act of diagnosis. As he methodically examines the patient and takes note of the symptoms, he is able to reach a conclusion that may not be initially obvious to the layperson. The doctor uses a number of diagnostic tools.

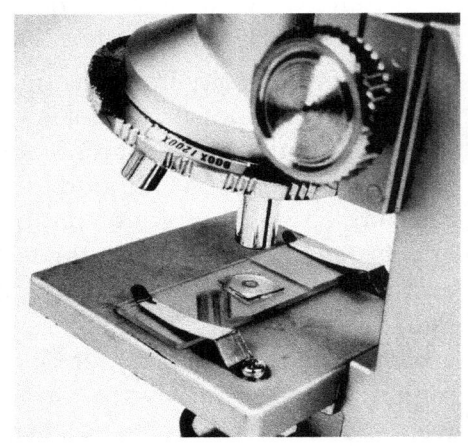

Similarly, the spiritual advisor uses a number of spiritual diagnostic tools.

Spiritual Warfare Expectations

As you embark on your journey as a 7M coach, you will undoubtedly experience new and even intense kinds of spiritual warfare that the intercessor will cover in prayer. WISE may sometimes need to call in the reinforcements—an extra intercessor or a spiritual coach, if you are a business or executive coach.

Know that the resistance will be broken.

If you are persistent and you ask the Lord for his wisdom, he will give it to you. Sin can profoundly affect the company and its people.

The SAT must work this out with the client with wisdom and in God's timing. Let the Lord speak to the client, and God will also speak to his leaders, if need be.

I cannot stress the importance of having a team plan which addresses every aspect of a business's present and future. As a coach, you get to present many of the plan's details to the client for his consideration, and you help him plan out his involement and the execution of the suggested plans.

Ten Things a Coach Can Do

Here are ten reasons you can give pre-clients to hire you:

CHECK YOUR ALIGNMENT. One of the first things that a good coach will do is make sure you are aimed at your target and that all of the fundamentals are sound. As your coach, I want to make sure that you have balance and that you are aligned with your purpose and connected with your calling.

CHECK YOUR BLINDSPOT. A coach can help you identify and remove some of the barriers you may have in place that are keeping you from achieving your goals and realizing your dreams.

CHECK YOUR PROGRESS. By having someone to check in with weekly, you have a new level of accountability. Reporting your accomplishments and initiatives to your coach keeps you focused on the small steps that are required to reach big results.

LIFE ENRICHMENT. There's more to life than work. A good coach can help you understand a life plan, reduce the stress in your life, build a fulfilling balance in your life, and improve your relationships with others. He can help improve your self-awareness and consciousness, improve your self-discipline, point you towards God and motivation, and even improve your health, well-being, and happiness.

CREATE YOUR VISION. Your coach can assist you in understanding your strengths and how to play to them. You have someone who can help you get very clear about who you are in God and your core values, passions, and needs.

CELEBRATION AND ENCOURAGEMENT. Your coach will celebrate with you as you accomplish and step toward your personal definition of success. There will be times when you'll need support, nurturing, and a source of energy to help you believe in yourself and achieve your dreams. A coach can help you turn setbacks into comebacks.

RAISING THE BAR. Constructive "challenge and stretch" goals can move you quickly to higher levels of achievement and prosperity. Your coach can identify new skills that you may need and provide you with resources and options for increasing your professional value.

COLLABORATOR AND CO-CONSPIRATOR. Imagine how much more confident you can be in your new ideas, creativity, and innovation when you've bounced them off a practiced, experienced professional who has worked through the challenges you are now facing. A coach is a sounding board and veteran who can show you the shortcuts he learned the hard way.

NONJUDGMENTAL. You can tell your coach anything, things you wouldn't tell anyone else. Your coach is trained to be nonjudgmental and objective. She'll point out where your thoughts aren't congruent with your goals or values, and will share where she has seen those ideas work or not. You can try out any thought or idea, and together you can find what's brilliant about it and get rid of the rest (within a biblical framework).

PLAYING THE BOUNCE. We live in times of incredible change. Life brings surprises, setbacks, changing circumstances, and economic realities. Technology is a game changer at every turn. Your coach can help you see the big picture—the effects on your industry and your clients—and help you prepare for, adjust during, and bounce back from difficult times.

Get Ready to Be a 7MCPC

Many times both I and my client have agendas, but Holy Spirit always has his agenda for the meeting.

We want to be sensitive to our clients' needs. They may have just been through a difficult situation and need to talk about it with us.

Many times the Lord will allow clients to be "triggered" so that the root cause of the issue can be healed and dealt with.

Get trained, but don't do this until God tells you that you are ready; stepping out too early could leave you open to spiritual attack. [Be sure to read the section on covering/alignment, because your alignment is critical for all who minister with a kingdom calling, especially coaches.]

Alignment is critical, and that is why God has brought WISE into your life. *How do you know when you are ready to step out and walk in this new authority?* Well, after you read this book and go through the class, you will be informed and up-to-date on what God is doing to empower leaders to fulfill their callings and to employ spiritual technologies and strategies. Jesus's death paid the price for them, and Holy Spirit has been sent to activate them on earth through you. Talk to your WISE representative and pray about the next steps.

How do you know when you are ready to step out? Well, after you read this book and go through the class, you may want to take an assignment with WISE (or another group that does professional coaching or intercession), or you may want to just start out on your own.

> Please be sure to go through the class if you want to start out on your own; it can literally save you thousands of dollars and jumpstart you into success by providing the WISE forms, contracts, letters, processes, and procedures you will need.

So again, how do you know you are ready? You may have the finances, the training, and even the moxy, but how do you know that you won't be beaten up in the spirit? When the seven sons of Sceva (Acts 19:13-16) were casting out evil spirits, one spirit said something very interesting: "Jesus I know, and Paul I know about, but who are you?" This was directly before they beat up the sons and tore their clothes off. The enemy knew the authority of Paul and of Jesus, but these sons of Sceva were not proven in spiritual warfare, nor in having knowledge of the Lord. The Lord asked Moses "'What is that in your hand?' 'A staff,' he replied" (Ex. 4:2). *Where is your staff?*

Is your name known in hell? Is your authority proven?

Is your ministry known in, say, counseling, chaplaincy, the prophetic, intercession, or deliverance?

What do you have to work with?

HAVE you assessed your strengths and weaknesses as a coach? The very fact that you have made it this far in this book is evidence of a high level of spiritual hunger (or perhaps desperation), inquisitiveness, and developing maturity.

WHAT gifts do you possess? What are your strengths? WISE staff can advise and assist you by guiding you through some of our master offerings, like making a DISC personality profile and helping you identify your spiritual gifts. As mentioned previously, we can also help increase your ability to hear God.

ARE you filled with the Spirit, with the evidence of speaking in tongues? Asked another way, do you have a prayer language? As I mentioned earlier in this book, the baptism in Holy Spirit is the gateway into the supernatural. Paul asked in Acts 19:1-2 "While Apollos was at Corinth, Paul took the road through the interior and arrived at Ephesus. There he found some disciples and asked them, 'Did you receive Holy Spirit when you believed?' They answered, 'No, we have not even heard that there is a Holy Spirit.'" (This is a subsequent and preferably coincidental experience. Ideally, right after someone is saved he can be filled with Holy Spirit, but in my case, I received the baptism a number of months later.)

HOW well do you hear God? Rate yourself on a scale of 1 to 10, with 1 being low and 10 being high on your ability to hear God. After coming on board with WISE, this number should increase. *We become like those we associate with.*

ARE you more apostolic or prophetic? Can you prophesy? This is not an absolute requirement, but it is very helpful. Are you willing to learn?

These and other questions need to be answered. Ask the Lord if you are ready. For many of you going through this book, the answer will be yes, and you will be delighted to have finally found a group like WISE to train and release you into this career and area of ministry.

If you do not feel ready, or if you do not have a peace, wait and continue to learn.

Go over this material again, but do not be afraid of the enemy's retaliation if you proceed. The enemy can smell fear and is attracted by it. Fear will be the greatest obstacle for you and any other believer to overcome. It is the opposite of faith.

Fear will test your faith; conversely, you fight fear with your faith. Remember, "God has allotted to each a measure of faith" (Rom. 12:3 NASB). This is the measure that you will need in order to function and do what God has called you to do. You already have the faith, just learn to apply it and, like Peter, walk on the water to Jesus, who is calling you.

Personal testimony - not being ready

> A personal testimony of when I was not ready: When Liz was pregnant with Nathanael, I was heaven-bent on starting a church out of our home. We were not attending church and I had no covering. We had a handful of people to whom I was preaching and ministering, but we experienced oppression and spiritual warfare at a level I was not used to. I was dealing with the territorial spirits in the Tampa Bay area and was not ready for that warfare. My supervisor had just told me that we were going to rewrite the system I had just spent eighteen months writing (as a computer programmer). Then Liz gave birth to Nathanael via a C-section and I had to take care of my new son. I was depressed; the church was not working. In addition, I was not sleeping. I felt alone. I remember complaining to the Lord, "No one believes in me." Right away the Lord said, "I believe in you!" Jesus came to me and said that he would never leave me. It was a great trial. It was during that time I experienced the benefit of one-on-one counseling. However, the little church folded. This experience helped me realize the importance of being properly aligned.

What Is Spiritual Alignment?

Favor is transferable. Who walks in the favor of God and understands your calling, gifts, strengths, and weaknesses?

Are you joined to and aligned with someone who has gone higher than you in God?

The kingdom of God is hierarchical; so is the kingdom of darkness. Both kingdoms operate in spheres of authority. They both recognize and respond to authority. There can only be one head in a spiritual structure. The authority of the head flows down to those who are under the head. Psalm 133:2 says "It is like precious oil poured on the head, running down on the beard, running down on Aaron's beard, down on the collar of his robe." My paraphrase: "It is like the oil that flows down Aaron's beard, down onto his garments, and there the Lord commands a blessing of unity."

The spiritual law at work here is that we become like those we associate with.

It is a *spiritual principle* that those who are aligned with or covered by an apostolic leader (very important) operate in the *same authority* of that leader. Put another way, those enemies who can be defeated by the apostolic leader can also be defeated by anyone aligned with that leader. Those enemies who come against anyone aligned with that leader also come against the leader himself. So there is the consideration of warfare from the leader's part as well, as far as who the leader is covering. The leader needs to know the people with whom he is aligning (whom the leader is covering) fairly well, otherwise he may experience unnecessary spiritual warfare from people who are not properly aligned with *God*.[*]

With whom are you aligned? Who is your apostle? Who can speak into your life, and who has gone further than you in the Spirit, not just in your specific calling as an intercessor? Who can break things off of you when you need it? Who knows your calling and gifting; who can bless and commission you? WISE can be that for you, or you may have someone else you trust. Just be sure to have this person (or persons) in your life, someone whom you can bounce ideas off. It may be a coach. Paul had Barnabas.

---

[*] I prefer the terms "alignment" over "covering" and "commissioning" over "ordination." A covering can become a smothering and has been abused in the past. Commissioning is a term I think is better than the word "ordained," since it carries with it an aspect of sending out, and a recognizing of not only the calling of God on a person, but also the location and specific assignment.

Chapter 7: Endnotes

Recommended Additional Resources for Readers and Students

Books

Vermaak, Natasha. *Repentance, Cleansing Your Generational Bloodline: Restoring the First Estate* (Vol. 1)

Hamon, Bill. *Apostles, Prophets, and the Coming Moves of God.*

Website articles

Mike Parsons, "Gateways of the Spirit," www.freedomarc.wordpress.com/2013/11/26/gateways-of-the-spirit

DVDs/CDs/MP3s

Robert Henderson, "Operating in the Courts of Heaven" (Parts 1-4), www.roberthenderson.org.

Ian Clayton, "Supernatural Encounters 101" conference set. www.resources.sonofthunder.org

People

Dutch Sheets, Dutch Sheets Ministries | dutchsheets.org

7M Strategies

The words were that God saw me as a knight in shining armor, and he was going to connect me with other significant people; I was going to have a turn of events and God was preparing a people for me to impart to and impact. That's the basis of the diagram, and I put it aside and went on with things, but at the same time Charles was saying to me multiple times to "hang in there until June; don't do anything drastic until June because something is going to happen in June."

What's happened is that your diagram was incredibly accurate! In retrospect it's amazing, and when I show it to people and give them the story behind it, the most common thing I hear is wow!

Here's what happened: We gathered all our forces and did a major effort to sell via our public seminars. To put this in perspective, three years ago we had approx. eight hundred people in these seminars, and this year the first six cities that we promoted in, which are cities where we have a good-standing client base, we had a total of one registration. It was clear that God was saying that it was time for this to be over. We couldn't have tried to do that badly! There was supernatural involvement in this. I saw this as the turn of events which you had drawn in your picture.

I began searching for something else to do, and asking God what he wanted me to do. I was led providentially to a group called "Truth at Work," which organizes Christian CEO round tables. We're now going to be doing a video webinar round table with Christian CEOs meeting on a monthly basis, helping them grow their businesses and develop spiritually. I am absolutely convinced that this is the fulfillment of the words that you wrote down about God preparing a significant people group for me to impart to and impact. So…this all happened in June! We're talking about working with CEOs of Christian businesses around the country, and maybe even around the world, in these webinars.

I'm just here thinking Wow! This is incredible!"

— Dave K., Comstock Park, MI

8

"He said, 'LORD, you are the God of our people. You are the God who is in heaven. You rule over all of the kingdoms of the nations. Your hands are strong and powerful. No one can fight against you and win.'... All of the kingdoms of the surrounding countries began to have respect for God. They had heard how the LORD had fought against Israel's enemies" (II Chronicles 20:6, 29 NIRV).

Strategic Intelligence to Take and Integrate All Seven Mountains

LET HEAVEN INVADE
THE SEVEN MOUNTAINS OF CULTURE

WISE is developing strategic intelligence to take and integrate all seven mountains together. This will result in further enabling the kingdom of God in the earth.

Each mountain needs a specific strategy

The strategy to advance a campaign on the government mountain is totally different than the one needed to produce a Christian film on the arts & entertainment mountain. You may, likewise, see differences for each mountain in the type and severity of spiritual warfare to expect and in the strategy needed to win the battle for culture.

One size definitely does not fit all when it comes to the strategies for intercession, coaching, and breakthrough. There are some universal strategies for all mountains; notably the strategy of using Scripture, because

God's Word always produces results.

Okay. *I admit,* I just told you one size does not fit all mountains for intercession, coaching, and breakthrough strategies, but then *I immediately changed course* to say that Scripture can be a starting point strategy to reclaim any mountain. Don't get distracted!

> *In the 7M certification course presentation, I will list the specific strategies and thoughts for each of the seven mountains. In no way will the list be exhaustive; it is, in fact, constantly developing as I travel, meet new clients, and encounter new situations. I will tell you that we have been involved in all seven mountains, so our experience is ongoing.*

Some general principles* may make what I say here resemble the lighthearted three-part sermon outline—"I'm gonna tell you what I'll

tell you, then I'll tell you, then I'll tell you what I told you." I've already stressed at least twice how important it is, as God's coach, to maintain an intimate walk with our Lord, and how he is the source to which you look for guidance for both you and your client's enterprise. In addition, you need to know how important these two spiritual disciplines are for you. When believers obey the truths in God's word, and seek him for guidance and direction, even just one or a small group can make a major impact!

Johnny Enlow says that the forces of darkness are at the summit of each of the seven mountains.†

> "Starting with Rosh Hashanah of 2015, a seismic shift will take place in the same way that the seven years of plenty ended in Egypt. If a great earthquake happens on that day, consider it the Lord's grace clearly signaling that earth-rattling changes

---

* In the *Change Agent* stories by Os Hillman
† See my friend Johnny Enlow's excellent book *The Seven Mountain Prophecy* and, for specific strategies for the mountains, see *The Seven Mountain Mantle,* also by J. Enlow.

are upon us. On this day, there will be a great unplugging of the systems of this world. The Lord will call for a famine on the foundations that are not sourced from His kingdom."

— Johnny Enlow, *The Seven Mountain Mantle*

Johnny says we will see the systematic crumbling of the systems of this world, and goes on to declare the need for the modern-day Josephs to arise with solutions to avert or lessen catastrophes. I see the times as being similar to those in Noah's day—God will depose the enemy's seven mountain leaders who are currently set up, and in their place set up his Josephs. It is a time for new beginnings.

Let us begin with how the seven mountains of culture are connected. The goal is to develop a strategy for each mountain or sphere that you may be operating in, and give you a strategy to connect those spheres or mountains when appropriate.

Defining 7M interconnections

Family is connected to all of the other mountains and is the foundation for everything because it is the most basic relational unit.

- Education and government are interconnected.
- Arts & entertainment and media are interconnected.
- Business and religion are interconnected—e.g., WISE.
- Business fuels all of the other mountains with finances.‡

We can see the sevenfold Spirit of the Lord reflected in these connections and, interestingly, could view these connections in the design of a menorah, where the middle candlestick is foundational and the other six candles are connected into pairs by the curved lines of the menorah.

As you review the connections between the seven mountains, in

---

‡ See Os Hillman's five-minute intro video about reclaiming the seven mountains, stressing the business mountain's strategic financial position, at www.7culturalmountains.org

light of the sevenfold spirit of the Lord in Isaiah 11:2, what does Holy Spirit say to you?

The Coming Seven Moves of God in the Mountains

The Lord has been speaking to me about the seven thunders in Revelation being connected to the seven mountains. The seven thunders are seven moves of God, one move related to each of the mountains. The scroll on which this was written was sealed up for the end times and then eaten by John; it was sweet to his mouth, but bitter to his stomach (see Rev. 10:9).

We are now in the days when the seventh angel is about to sound his trumpet! "Then the voice that I had heard from heaven spoke to me once more: 'Go, take the scroll that lies open in the hand of the angel who is standing on the sea and on the land'" (Rev. 10:8). The angel was standing on the sea (indicting humanity) and the land (indicating the marketplace). This is a move to *connect* the people to the marketplace and to *complete* the final work of God.

Notice there is a *last days prophetic movement* coming which is related to the voice of the seven thunders, the content of which was *sealed up.*

The message of God in our day will be sweet (because we are speaking the exhilarating and fresh words of the Lord to each mountain) but in the outworking of it, the *digesting* of it, if you will. We—as God's Josephs—will have to endure the many shakings that are coming upon the world (but we will be victorious).

As the message continues in Revelation 10:11, "Then I was told, you must prophesy again about many peoples, nations, languages and kings." Notice many peoples (out of the sea), nations (sheep nations), languages and *kings* (indicating the marketplace). These seven end-time messages will be sent *to the entire earth* and to *all seven mountains of influence.*

Finally, John was given a reed and told to measure the temple (the religion mountain) (see Rev. 11:1). The implication is that this event was next in the sequence, *but it may not be.* My opinion is that it *is* next in the sequence of chronological events. The religion mountain is very important to God.

The book of Revelation next mentions the two witnesses. Their power is to defy death and to exact the wrath of God on the earth during the great tribulation, but there must be a move of God in each mountain beforehand! Maybe God will use *you* to prophesy and release one or more of these seven thundering voices, which are seven moves of God—one for each sphere or mountain of influence. Like John I say, "Even so, come quickly, Lord Jesus!"

The Tipping Point

Since 2000, Lance Wallnau§ and Os Hillman¶ have given many talks about the marketplace ministry strategy for taking the seven mountains (and have been talking about it more since 2009). Christians who desire to reform our culture have changed their strategies in order to honor the tipping point. Early on, the strategy focused on placing Christians at high points—points of leadership (affluence and/or influence)—in the seven mountains. A weakness of that strategy was that it could be a slow process (and often quite expensive) to place only a few leaders in high places. We noticed that the morality of a company (or segment of society, such as a city agency) could not be dictated downward to those working at lower positions.

Another aspect of societal change offers more promise for easier and, perhaps, faster results—the aspect of a tipping point. Missionaries have observed this phenomenon. Although it takes only a small percentage (4 percent) of leaders to create an appreciable influence on a segment of society, it doesn't take much more of the grassroots population (a little over 10 percent) to influence one. Currently, those Christians who desire to reform all seven segments (mountains) of society are shifting their foci to concentrate on creating tipping points. They are focused now on making more disciples at

---

§ Find more info on Lance Wallnau at www.lancelearning.biz.
¶ Find more info on Os Hillman at www.marketplaceleaders.org.

the grass roots level on each mountain rather than placing a few Christians in high areas of affluence and influence. The result can be to, essentially, tip the mountain over through the influence of that critical percentage of Christians exerting their grass roots influence (enhanced by the spiritual power of our Creator).

What does 7-UP have to do with a tipping point? Well, picture in your mind the seven mountains of culture (business, education, media, etc.) tipped over so that the playing field of each mountain (the base) is now at the top, and a base of Christians have access to the mountain peak, not just the top influencers. We are turning things upside-down (right-side up), hence the term "7-UP."

How can a 7M coach interact with that strategy? God can use any business or enterprise as a change agent to help reform society. For instance, as you mentor on godly time management, your client places his first priority on quality time spent with God (which helps bring the insight and blessings God has intended from the religion mountain for him and his business, and empowers his success). As he places his second priority on time spent with his spouse, and his third priority on time spent with his children, he honors God in a way that creates ripples of blessing in the family mountain. As he continues to align his priorities with God's priorities, he puts his organization at the next (fourth) area of priority, which is in the proper position to receive the tangible and spiritual blessings God ordains for his business. Your coaching and mentorship increase the spiritual power at work in this process.

What is a tipping point?

What is a tipping point? A critical juncture, a defining moment in a series of events (think economic, cultural, social, etc.,) at which time a series of significant, often momentous and irreversible, reactions occur. We are at many tipping points in society: governmental, financial, economic, spiritual, etc.[1]

You were created to be a world changer and history maker. You are needed.

Transformation

The Lord is raising up modern-day Josephs and Daniels and those like the sons of Issachar who "knew what the times demanded" (I Chron. 12:32). We believe that God's angels and anointing will be available to strengthen and empower you to finish the race that is before you.

God can show you the technology, healing, demographics, and spiritual waves that are coming and how to respond to them to get his people ready. He is going to show you the new economic super cycles that are coming, the new trends, and new inventions.

A major blessing an SAT can be to the business community is in its ability to help each owner transform his enterprise into a kingdom company. WISE can partner with your client to create a kingdom company and bring it everything it needs to function in its destiny. You are one of the Josephs and Daniels of the twenty-first century and we are here to serve you.

Now your client's business has the opportunity to be realigned from its foundations up, and you may influence an enterprise that can serve and change the nations.

Chapter 8: Endnotes

1. Gladwell, Malcolm. *The Tipping Point: How Little Things Can Make a Big Difference.* New York: Back Bay Books, 2002.

Recommended Additional Resources for Readers/Students

Books

Hillman, Os. *Change Agent: Engaging Your Passion to Be the One Who Makes a Difference* [which contains a chapter for reclaiming each of the seven mountains, and relates stories of successful culture change, often by a single change agent or small group, and the strategies used to accomplish those successes].

Enlow, Johnny. *The Seven Mountain Mantle*

Ferguson, David. *Top 10 Intimacy Needs* (Intimacy Monograph Series)

Femrite, Tommi. *Invading the Seven Mountains With Intercession: How to Reclaim Society Through Prayer*

Wallnau, Lance, and Bill Johnson. *Invading Babylon: The 7 Mountain Mandate*

DVDs/CDs/MP3s

Os Hillman. "Reclaiming the 7 Mountains of Culture Introduction." DVD. www.tgifbookstore.com.

Lance Wallnau. "The 7 Mountain Mandate: Impacting Culture Discipling Nations." DVD. www.morningstarministries.org.

Os Hillman, Lance Wallnau, Johnny Enlow, and others. "7 Mountain Strategies: Keys for Cultural Influence." Audio CD Series. www. tgifbookstore.com

Website articles

Os Hillman, TGIF Daily Marketplace Devotional, www.marketplaceleaders.org/tgif

Videos

www.TippingPoint.TV

People

Os Hillman, Marketplace Leaders
www.marketplaceleaders.org
and his TGIF bookstore www.tgifbookstore.com

YOUR CHOICES

"I have been blessed with WISE Marketplace Ministries. I have enjoyed our prayer times, meetings, and prophetic words. I also have been blessed by the intercessor who was assigned to us and the details of her prayer times, which she e-mailed to us. This has blessed me to see the type of prayer going on behind the scenes. May God richly bless WISE and open new doors to new businesses."

— Daniel G., Austin, TX

"Charles and Liz have played a major intercessory role in my personal journey. In this end-time season, it is absolutely critical that the arrows of intercession we shoot hit the mark all the time."

— Patrick Kuwana
Founder, Crossover Transformation Group
Johannesburg, South Africa

9

WISE Ministries International

WISE Ministries International is helping birth the spiritual services industry. It is a pioneer in the new "strategic intelligence" space, otherwise called "coaching and intercession for enterprises." Dr. Charles and Liz Robinson founded WISE Ministries International in 2005 to be a training, equipping, and service ministry to businesses, ministries, and enterprises in all seven mountains of culture. WISE provides intercession, kingdom consulting, and timely prophetic words in all seven of the spheres of culture, sometimes referred to as the seven mountains of culture: business, government, arts & entertainment, media, education, family, and religion. WISE services provide a vibrant training, consulting, and healing ministry for developing and equipping the body of Christ to live in victory through experiencing the delivering power of Jesus Christ, our Lord and Savior. WISE teaches people how to incorporate prayer into their enterprises, and trains and imparts into the next generation.

WISE is active in:

Government - by supporting local and national candidates, by impacting the governmental mountain through DC-based intercessory teams, and through its Gates2DC.com ministry;

Arts & Entertainment - through the Gates2Hollywood.com ministry and association with several major Christian film studios and releases;

Family - through its marriage counseling ministry;

Education - through its ministry at foundational universities, such as Harvard University;

Business - through entrance, via intercession and/or coaching, into over one hundred companies in numerous industries;

Religion - through support of church and parachurch ministries; and

Media - via Internet; via satellite—the On The Way Network and

Cross Network, which covers the globe, with access to over 120 million people.

WISE employs intercessors and coaches all over the world in a decentralized model, utilizing the latest in Internet technologies, to teach people how to incorporate prayer into their enterprises.

WISE maintains offices in Hollywood, California; Austin, Texas; and Washington, D.C.; and we can also travel to enterprises for on-site initial consultations, assessments, and evaluations.

Licensing and Commissioning Leaders in the Marketplace

As a part of *our* commissioning, we (WISE) license and commission (we formerly used the word ordain) leaders in the marketplace. WISE recognizes that God has called leaders in all the seven mountains, not just in the religious mountain.

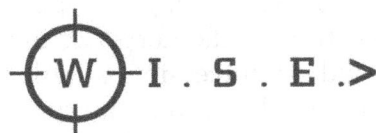

Workplace. Intercession. Support. Empowerment.™
Focused and Targeted Strategic Intelligence

Accordingly, WISE recognizes that these ministers do not differ to God in importance as compared to those who hold traditional ministry positions in church, or who are supported by the church, such as missionaries. WISE further recognizes that those who have the ministry gift of apostle, prophet, pastor, etc. can function in their spheres of influence, i.e., in one or more of the seven mountains. WISE recognizes how vital it is, as a person progresses in his spiritual calling, to have a person or a group honor him and acknowledge his authority and sphere of influence by setting him in or consecrating him and being there as a guiding hand. If you or a leader you know could benefit from licensing (which is akin to a dating period for one year) or from commissioning, please contact our office to receive a list of requirements and benefits.

The Need for Training and Certification

I am certified, but the certification did not cost $10,000 - $15,000, which some accrediting organizations charge. Our own, granted, is not cheap. Go with someone you trust. Is becoming a John Maxwell Certified Coach for you? Is certification with the International Coaching Federation (ICF) for you? There is value in all of these. I am a testament that you do not need expensive certifications (but again, they may be worth it for you).

When I am coached, I do not want John, as good as he is in leadership. I want Jesus. I want to hear what heaven is saying. When God coaches through me, he does not want me to follow someone else's prescription, he wants me to be me—empowered by his Spirit.

Being you is good enough.

You, in God's moment and empowered by his Spirit, can relate exactly what heaven wants for your client in any situation—no matter which type of coach you are. Use your training and then ask God to help you.

As a prophetic business coach, I remember being brought into a situation. This new client flew me out to his home in Alabama and paid me well to answer one question. He was a day trader, and he went on vacation and committed the one cardinal sin in stock trading—he missed his stops. He had set "stop losses" in his mind but not in real life. He was trading the S&P 500 index, and was thinking about either staying in or closing out his position. He was at the edge of losing around $150,000, and if he made a wrong move, that chunk of money was lost. Talk about being put on the spot! It was noon and the index was going down a little every few minutes. Every time it went down a pip, he lost more money, so in essence, his entire investment was potentially at risk. He was perspiring and asked me what God wanted him to do. Talk about being under pressure!

I asked the Lord and he told me that the index would not continue to go down and that it would revive during the afternoon. This sweaty man took a sigh of relief and did not exit his positions. Sure enough the price recovered that afternoon to close. There is no coaching certification in the world, at any price, that would have taught me that. Only the relationship that I had with God got me out of that situation. Sounds like something that Joseph in the Bible would do—the solving of enigmas. Being unable to answer these types of questions caused the magicians in Joseph's day to bite the dust.

There is nothing like the feeling of seeing the light go on, the tears flow, and the look of delight on a client's face. All he needs is you! Every coach is different, so let your unique gift mix and life experiences flow. This is not rocket science. Some of you are making this more difficult than it really is. The masters in any discipline make it look easy because they do what they love, what comes naturally, what they were created to do. Remember that epic line in the *Chariots of Fire* film? "When I run, I feel his pleasure?"

> *Feel God's pleasure in your coaching; enjoy every moment.*

WISE provides a wide range of courses in personal development to WISE clients—in person, by telephone, SKYPE, and/or e-mail correspondence—through life, spiritual, and executive coaching in various areas and levels. We also offer courses for business transformation, and on how to assist leaders through transitions. WISE also offers personal ministry using spiritual and relational tools.

Certification Courses

WISE currently offers four certification courses in a series called "Let Heaven Invade the Seven Mountains of Culture."

WISE 7M Intercessor Certification trains those with a calling to intercessory prayer to become seven mountains professional level intercessors.

WISE 7M Leadership Certification informs leaders how to identify, engage, manage, and release intercessors, corporate pastors, spiritual coaches, and chief revelatory officers into their organizations for their corporate and personal well-being.[*]

WISE 7M Coaches Certification (spiritual coach, life coach, executive coach, and executive leadership coach options).[†]

WISE 7M Chaplain Certification is for corporate pastors or chaplains called to minister to an organization's employees.[‡]

WISE 7M Generals Certification is for the top 7M marketplace leaders who need to deal with (take authority over and get to the root of) many situations which can arise in their global enterprises.[§]

---

[*] See marketplaceCEOS.com for more information.
[†] See marketplacecoaches.com for more information.
[‡] See corporatepastors.com for more information.
[§] See marketplacecoaches.com for more information.

Course schedule and format options

Certification courses happen monthly. All four of the courses listed above are available in two formats:

Group and Fast Track: Two-and-a-half days of live on-site training

Independent Study: All modules are divided over twelve weeks.

Both formats offer wisdom and experience from WISE instructors.

Why certify as a WISE leader?

Reading this guide without participating in a live class or recorded sessions will prove to be valuable; however, if you wish to receive certification and full impartation (including proprietary material, sample forms and processes, etc.), you will need to attend the classes, or at least view the recorded version of the classes and complete the exercises.

You will be able to fully utilize and understand WISE's master offerings for you, your family, and your organization(s). Most importantly, certification will educate you on getting the most out of the spiritual services industry that WISE is helping to birth.

We hope you will align with us to see your destiny come forth.

Option 1: WISE Certifies You and Refers Clients to You as a WISE 7MCPC

You attend our certification class, either in person or online, and sign our nondisclosure agreement when you receive your course material (since in your class you will receive many forms which are the intellectual property of WISE).

We work together. You can utilize our front-end (initial consult) process, our back office (invoicing and accounts receivable), receive referrals from us, know exactly how we charge, be able to offer your clients all of our master offerings, etc., and have my ongoing mentoring (even after you are certified as a coach).

There is no charge for this other than the charge for the certification class. We both make money on an ongoing basis. You represent WISE; we refer clients to you (based upon availability), you refer clients to us, and you are their coach. (WISE staff will review the compensation plan with you.)

There are numerous proprietary details at this stage of the course that I teach you. This option means that in regards to coaching, you will become a part of WISE and will not be doing your own thing. You need to think about this. With the 7MCPC certification curriculum, I teach you how to do what we do.

Option 1 is the closest possible connection to WISE you can have.

Remember, there is no charge to be a WISE 7MCPC, but if you prefer to run your own independent coaching practice, you'll want to choose option 2.

With option 1, as a WISE 7MCPI, you will also sign a two-year non-compete agreement, which basically means that you agree, upon separation from WISE, to not compete directly with us for a duration of two years (when and even if that happens; hopefully we will be working together until the rapture or the second coming, depending on your eschatology!).

Compensation Expectations for Option 1:

WISE will negotiate you an appropriate rate (see below). This is usually 50-75 percent of our billing rate, but depends on who brought in the client.

Option 2: WISE Certifies You as a 7MCPC and Licenses You as an Independent CPC

You attend our certification class, either in person or online, and sign our nondisclosure agreement when you receive your course material (since in the class you will receive many forms which are the intellectual property of WISE).

You do the work, benefit from your connection with us, and conform to the standards required in bearing the WISE name. I license you to do what we do. (You do not need to bear our name if you want to have your own name, BTW, but there is value and brand recognition with our name, which has been building since 2005.)

With option 2, you become a certified 7MCPC and you will be

connected to WISE, but your business will be independent of WISE. Being a certified and licensed WISE coach, you get to use the WISE name and logo—everything—or your own, whichever you prefer. You become an extension of us yet build your business independently, keep all the money, and have access to all of our methods and processes and procedures on an ongoing basis. When we receive a breakthrough technique, strategy, etc., you receive it too because you are a part of WISE.

Picture it as similar to your starting a McDonald's, except you are purchasing a WISE license rather than a McDonald's franchise. This option requires an up-front cost and an annual fee (after the first year) for ongoing support, which includes a two-day on-site visit for one-on-one training in marketing, e-mail marketing, website setup and design—everything you need to get you started on the fast track. [We have developed and refined our processes since 2005, and have ministered in over one hundred companies. We are pioneers in this field in many ways.] Contact WISE for the current license fee and yearly maintenance fee.

Compensation Expectations for Option 2:

You get to keep all of your fees. Contact WISE for infomation on how we can help suport the office end of your independent business.

Think of this license option as going into business for yourself but not by yourself. With the 7MCPC certification, I teach you how to do what we do [but option 1 helps you go to a greater depth than with option 2. Remember, there is no charge to be a WISE 7MCPC, but it is exclusive of your doing your own independent coaching and business administration (option 2)].

Option 3: You Read the Text Only and Are an Independent Coach - Not Certified by Us

You do the work. You read the course manual. You do not receive the forms that are the intellectual property of WISE. You do not sign a nondisclosure agreement. With this subset of what we do, you can run your own coaching business independently of WISE. You can contact WISE if you wish to purchase consulting services about questions you might have, such as how much to charge, what to do in specific situations, how WISE can assist you in ministering to your challenging client, etc.

Note that with options 1 and 2, I teach about the coaching profession and pepper it with some of the processes, forms, and procedures that we use at WISE so you can be successful on your own. I can also train you in the WISE way so that you can be connected with WISE in greater depth—to become a WISE 7MCPC (option 1); or go through certification as a 7MCPC, purchase a license, and maintain an ongoing connection with our methods, processes, and procedures (option 2).

The bottom line for option 3 is this: I won't give everything away if you are going to do your own thing and compete with us using our own methods.

Other ways to earn income with WISE

WISE has many courses in our ever-expanding master offerings list, but we require you to be licensed with us in order for you to offer them to your clients. Charles and Liz will personally work out an agreement with you that will be financially beneficial to both you and WISE. Contact WISE staff for more information on how to acquire a current complete list of offerings and fees.¶

A Changing Church

Many people's coverings are beginning to come off. This is a good thing. Last year I saw people moving to many new assignments and moving geographically, as we did ourselves. Now I see, as it were, people wrapped up as a gift in wrapping paper. The wrapping paper represents your current spiritual coverings. It's colorful and there is much variety, but it's thin in its manufacture. The wrapping paper would tear easily after some handling it. It was not meant to contain you but to present you (get it, a present, as a gift)? The wrapping paper was covering up the gift(s) that God's people have. The wrapping paper represents denominations or other ministry groups that have served their purposes. God is taking the wraps off and exposing you and your ministry in a new way. It is time for your gifts to come forward. The wraps are coming off. God is letting the cat out of the bag. Get ready to burst onto the scene and for your exposure

---

¶ http://coachmybusiness.com/contact.php

to the world—the special gift that you are and the gifts you possess. Your covering served a purpose for a season, but now it is changing.

Business:

I see new opportunities for kingdom businesses. Do not let fear hold you back. There are new opportunities for you to branch into. I see the word *burst* and a burst of activity for some businesses that are positioned to benefit from new markets, products, and service lines. Stand still and you will lose ground. Build the infrastructure to handle the increase of activity you're going to see. Counteract fear with faith and intimacy with God. Get closer to him, rededicate your business to him, and the sky is the limit!

This is the year in which nothing is impossible, and impossible is nothing.

About the Author

Dr. Charles and Liz Robinson have pioneered a global breakthrough in marketplace ministry through WISE Ministries International—a ministry that empowers leaders by providing a combination of business, spiritual, and prophetic support—using their impressive history of degrees and experience as a foundational guide. Both ordained ministers with the CIAN, and as current directors of the IAMIN, Charles and Liz maintain offices in Austin, Hollywood, and Washington, D.C. in order to personally minister on the mountains of business, entertainment, and government.

Charles is also the convener of the bi-annual Tipping Point Gathering 7-UP Unconference—an interactive three-day meeting of key leaders from the seven mountains of influence.

More From WISE Ministries

WISE Prayer Request Website and Theme song
WISE Prayer request site and theme song: www.coachmybusiness.com/prayer-request.php

WISE Online Store Links for DVDs
DVDs from WISE (provided to Certification Course Students):

Intercession 2.0 http://tinyurl.com/k6fcsbu

Taking Company to Next Level Spiritually http://tinyurl.com/otbal4n

Opening Global Gates of Access and Provision http://tinyurl.com/ope7kn9

Tipping Point Media from WISE online store
Tipping Point 2013 Gathering Conference DVD (also available on CD and MP3) http://tinyurl.com/oxmvg58

Our iPhone/Android Mobile App

As you move forward with your relationship with WISE, use our WISE app to submit your prayer requests, read our blog, find out where our next gatherings are going to be, or receive a prophetic word.

WISE Ministries International websites

Our main prayer websites:
sites:
    prayformybusiness.com
    prayformyministry.com

Our 7M sites:
tippingpointgathering.com
7mcouncil.com
charlesrobinson.com
7minstitute.com
josephregistry.com

Our intercessor certification

    IAMCERT.com
    marketplaceintercessors.com

Our coaching sites:
coach4mylife.com
marketplacecoaches.com
coachmybusiness.com^2
marketplacegenerals.com
marketplacepastors.com

WISE provides monthly newsletters in "The Joseph Blog," available at:

coachmybusiness.com/marketplace-ministry

The 7M book series is available at the site:

www.letheaveninvade7m.com

For information and to register for monthly gatherings, visit:

www.tippingpointnw.com

Site to purchase *Let Heaven Invade the Seven Mountains of Culture*:

www.letheaveninvade7m.com

www.ingramcontent.com/pod-product-compliance
Lightning Source LLC
Chambersburg PA
CBHW070921160426
43193CB00011B/1545